MODERN MASTERS

MANET to

MATISSE

MODERN MASTERS

MANET to MATISSE

THE MUSEUM
of MODERN ART
NEW YORK

EDITED by
WILLIAM S.
LIEBERMAN

An exhibition organized under the auspices of The International Council of The Museum of Modern Art, New York

Schedule of the Exhibition: Art Gallery of New South Wales, Sydney, April 10-May 11, 1975. National Gallery of Victoria, Melbourne, May 28-June 22, 1975. The Museum of Modern Art, New York, August 4-September 1, 1975.

Designed by Carl Laanes. Published by The Museum of Modern Art, 11 West 53 Street, New York, New York 10019. All rights reserved. Printed by Norman J. Field & Co. Pty. Ltd., Melbourne

cover   MATISSE: *The Young Sailor.* 1906. Oil on canvas, 39⅜ x 31⅞". Collection Mr. and Mrs. Jacques Gelman, Mexico City

frontispiece   MANET: *Women at the Races.* 1865. Oil on canvas, 16⅝ x 12⅝". Cincinnati Art Museum

THIS CATALOG AND THE exhibition it accompanies have been prepared under the auspices of The International Council of The Museum of Modern Art, New York, and have been made possible by the generous assistance and support of the Australian Council for the Arts and of Alcoa Foundation.

LENDERS TO THE EXHIBITION

E. M. Bakwin

Dr. Ruth M. Bakwin

Mrs. William A. Bernoudy

Edward A. Bragaline

Mr. and Mrs. Gordon Bunshaft

Mrs. Gilbert W. Chapman

Mr. and Mrs. Ralph F. Colin

Mr. and Mrs. Allan D. Emil

Mr. and Mrs. Victor W. Ganz

Mr. and Mrs. Jacques Gelman

Dr. Armand Hammer

Lady Harlech

Mr. and Mrs. Henry J. Heinz II

Mr. and Mrs. Alex M. Lewyt

Dr. and Mrs. Barnett Malbin

Mr. and Mrs. David Rockefeller

Mr. and Mrs. Alexandre P. Rosenberg

Mrs. Bertram Smith

Mr. and Mrs. Donald S. Stralem

Harry Torczyner

Mr. and Mrs. Burton Tremaine

Mrs. Lloyd Bruce Wescott

Mr. and Mrs. John Hay Whitney

Richard S. Zeisler

Twelve anonymous collectors

The Baltimore Museum of Art

Museum of Fine Arts, Boston

The Brooklyn Museum

Albright-Knox Art Gallery, Buffalo

The Art Institute of Chicago

Cincinnati Art Museum

The Cleveland Museum of Art

The Detroit Institute of Arts

Wadsworth Atheneum, Hartford

The Tate Gallery, London

National Gallery of Victoria, Melbourne

Milwaukee Art Center

Yale University Art Gallery, New Haven

The Solomon R. Guggenheim Museum, New York

The Metropolitan Museum of Art, New York

The Museum of Modern Art, New York

Whitney Museum of American Art, New York

Musée National d'Art Moderne, Paris

Philadelphia Museum of Art

The Art Museum, Princeton University

The St. Louis Art Museum

Marion Koogler McNay Art Institute, San Antonio

San Francisco Museum of Art

Norton Gallery of Art, West Palm Beach

Sterling and Francine Clark Art Institute, Williamstown

IN ITS SUPPORT OF THE arts, Alcoa Foundation seeks discriminating and innovative approaches to provide the world community with opportunities to see, enjoy, and appreciate fine art. Sponsorship of The Museum of Modern Art's exhibition of *Modern Masters: Manet to Matisse* gives us a unique opportunity to offer the public in Australia and the United States the pleasure of viewing masterpieces gathered from both public and private collections throughout the world. It is an honor to be associated with The Museum of Modern Art, its International Council, and the Australian Council for the Arts in this program. The directors of Alcoa Foundation hope the pleasure this exhibition brings to the public will equal our pleasure in helping to make it possible.

A. M. Doty, President
Alcoa Foundation

CONTENTS

FOREWORD 10

PREFACE 13

COLOR PLATES 15

IMPRESSIONISM 35

POST-IMPRESSIONISM 55

MATISSE 83

EXPRESSIONISM IN
FRANCE AND
GERMANY 107

CUBISM AND ITS
AFFINITIES 137

THE PAINTED DREAM 175

TEN PORTRAITS 205

THE SCHOOL OF
PARIS: TEN
PAINTERS 227

CATALOG 261

ACKNOWLEDGMENTS 270

THIS EXHIBITION of paintings by masters of the modern tradition is one of the most ambitious ever sent abroad by The Museum of Modern Art. It has been organized under the auspices of the Museum's International Council in response to requests of many years' standing from Australian museums for a major presentation of some of the key developments in modern art. It is a tribute to the current status of the arts in Australia that what for so long seemed a visionary project can now be realized.

As director of *Modern Masters: Manet to Matisse*, William S. Lieberman, Director of the Museum's Department of Drawings, has demonstrated his superb knowledge and judgment in selecting the exhibition, as well as an extraordinary persuasiveness in obtaining the consent of the many lenders to part with important works for an extensive period of time. Monroe Wheeler, an Honorary Trustee of The Museum of Modern Art and a member of the International Council, graciously consented to be Honorary Chairman of the exhibition.

The exhibition has been made possible through the enlightened support of the Australian Council for the Arts and through a most generous grant from Alcoa Foundation. For an exhibition of this magnitude, involving loans of more than one hundred major works from outstanding private and public collections, the cost of fine arts insurance would have been prohibitive. Indeed, but for the agreement of the Commonwealth of Australia to assume responsibility for the risks ordinarily covered by private insurance, the exhibition could never have been undertaken. Long urged by museums throughout the world, and pioneered by the government of Great Britain, such indemnity agreements are among the most significant means by which governments can assist museums in organizing important international loan exhibitions.

In addition to providing indemnification, the Australian government has underwritten many of the costs of the exhibition. We want to express our warm appreciation to the Right Honorable E.G. Whitlam, Prime Minister of Australia, both for the personal interest he has shown in the present exhibition and for his distinguished role in furthering government aid for the arts. Our gratitude is also extended to His Excellency Sir Patrick Shaw, Australian Ambassador to the United States, and General Sir John Wilton, Australian Consul General in New York, for their assistance in coordinating many arrangements for the exhibition.

Much of the administrative organization has been effectively handled by the Visual Arts Board of the Australian Council for the Arts. Special gratitude is owed to Dr. Jean Battersby, Executive Officer of the Council, and to John Baily, Chairman of the Visual Arts Board, for their support of the project from the outset. Leon Paroissien, Director of the Visual Arts Board, and Klaus Kuziow, Exhibitions Officer, traveled to

FOREWORD

the United States to collaborate with the Museum staff on complex organizational details and have worked tirelessly on the exhibition's behalf.

Many members of the staff of the Australian state galleries in Sydney and Melbourne have participated in the planning and presentation of the exhibition. We wish especially to thank Peter Laverty, Director of the Art Gallery of New South Wales, and Gil Docking, its Deputy Director; and Gordon Thomson, Director of the National Gallery of Victoria, and Kenneth Hood, Deputy Director. We are also grateful to Eric Westbrook, Director, Victorian Ministry for the Arts, whose advice and assistance have been particularly helpful.

The exhibition also would not have been possible without the assistance provided by Alcoa Foundation, which has long been an innovative leader of corporate support of the arts. In 1970, Alcoa Foundation aided the presentation of *Four Americans in Paris: The Collections of Gertrude Stein and Her Family*. We are once again deeply grateful for the extraordinarily generous grant of Alcoa Foundation to *Modern Masters: Manet to Matisse*, and we warmly acknowledge the initiative of its directors in supporting cultural exchange between the United States and Australia. We thank in particular Arthur M. Doty, President of Alcoa Foundation, for the conviction and enthusiasm he has brought to the project, and Krome George, President and Chief Executive Officer of Aluminum Company of America, for his active interest and support.

The International Council of The Museum of Modern Art, under whose auspices the exhibition has been organized, comprises a group of art patrons from many parts of the United States and twenty foreign countries. The Council's six Australian members deserve special mention for their invaluable assistance: The Lady Casey, James Fairfax, Mrs. Chester Guest, Mrs. John D. Lewis, Mrs. M. A. McGrath, and Mrs. Harry Seidler. Mrs. Alfred R. Stern, President of the Council, has aided immeasurably in plans for the exhibition, as has Mrs. Burton Tremaine, founding Chairman of the Australian Committee. Mrs. John D. Rockefeller 3rd, the first President of the Council and now the President of the Museum, has been unfailingly supportive.

The Museum seldom has the opportunity to present to the public in New York exhibitions it has organized for circulation abroad. It is therefore especially gratifying that the exhibition will be shown in our own galleries after the presentations in Sydney and Melbourne. We are confident that the exhibition will not only give pleasure to our many visitors but also create a greater awareness of the Museum's extensive international program of cultural exchange in the visual arts.

Richard E. Oldenburg, Director, The Museum of Modern Art
August Heckscher, Chairman, The International Council of The Museum of Modern Art

VAN GOGH: *Street at Sainte-Maries*. 1888.

Brush, reed pen and ink, traces of pencil, 9⅝ x 12½".   The Museum of Modern Art, New York. Abby Aldrich Rockefeller Bequest

PREFACE

MODERN MASTERS, as an exhibition, surveys almost a century of European painting which starts with Manet in 1861 and closes soon after the death of Matisse in 1954. The selection has been conceived in eight chapters: Impressionism; Post-Impressionism; Matisse, in a sequence of eleven examples; Expressionism, including the Fauve painters in France and the members of the Bridge and Blue Rider in Germany; Cubism, in France, and its affinities in Italy, Germany, and Russia; the "painted dream," which in this exhibition refers to painters of fantasy before, during, and after Surrealism; portraits, a personal predilection; and, last, a brief summary in significant examples of the work of ten painters of the School of Paris which begins with Bonnard's *Boulevard de Clichy* in 1900 and ends with Picasso's climactic version of his *Women of Algiers*.

The exhibition has been organized for two museums in Australia, which, like tomorrow, is very near but also very far. With the exception of three works on paper, which are vulnerable to continued exposure to light, the selection will subsequently be shown in New York.

As always, I am beholden to friends. First, I acknowledge with gratitude the thirty-six collectors who have so graciously surrendered from their homes for so long a time some of their most cherished possessions, paintings from which they derive daily sustenance and pleasure. Second, and equally, I acknowledge the collaboration of colleagues at museums in France, Great Britain, and the United States as well as in Australia. Directors of museums and curators of collections have responded warmly to the challenge of the exhibition and have temporarily surrendered custody of forty-five paintings so that they can be shared with a new audience on a different continent.

Six months has been a short time to harvest the selection of such paintings. Only with the cooperation and professional skill of two associates at the Museum, Monawee A. Richards and John Stringer, has this been possible.

I want also to thank Hubert Landais, Assistant to the Director of the Museums of France, Dominique Bozo, Chief Curator at the Musée National d'Art Moderne, Paris, Richard S. Zeisler, Chairman of the Program Committee of the International Council, Monroe Wheeler, an Honorary Trustee of The Museum of Modern Art as well as a participant in its International Council, and Waldo Rasmussen, Director of the International Program. Seminal discussions with all five preceded the selection of the exhibition which began in September.

In addition, I wish to express thanks for special assistance to Mr. and Mrs. Alfred H. Barr, Jr., Mr. and Mrs. Heinz Berggruen, Mr. and Mrs. Ralph F. Colin, Mme

Marcel Duchamp, Mr. and Mrs. Victor W. Ganz, Mr. and Mrs. Jacques Gelman, Mrs. Cecil Blaffer Hudson, Mrs. Fernand Leval, Mr. and Mrs. Pierre Matisse, Sir Roland and Lady Penrose, Mr. and Mrs. John D. Rockefeller 3rd, Mr. and Mrs. Wolfgang Schoenborn, Mr. and Mrs. Charles G. Stachelberg, and Mr. and Mrs. Eugene Victor Thaw.

At the Museum, in addition to Mrs. Richards and Mr. Stringer, both of whom worked unstintingly in addition to their usual assigned responsibilities, I wish to thank Susana Leval, Lisa Messenger, Laura Rosenstock, Cora Rosevear, Eric Rowlison, Richard Tooke, and Patricia White. The Department of Publications was obliged to initiate production of the exhibition's catalog before final negotiations for loans had been completed. Mary Lea Bandy, Jack Doenias, and Carl Laanes responded resourcefully and with patience to this difficult circumstance.

Once again, it has been a pleasure to work with Alcoa Foundation, whose generous and enthusiastic support of the arts has made possible this exhibition.

W.S.L.

COLOR PLATES

TOULOUSE-LAUTREC:
M. Boileau in a Café.
1893. See page 208

opposite   RENOIR:
Monet Painting in His Garden.
c. 1874. See page 42

MONET: *Still Life With a
Basket of Eggs.* c. 1910.
See page 52

CEZANNE: *Mme Cézanne
in a Yellow Chair.*
1893-95. See page 64

DERAIN: *Henri Matisse.*
1905. See page 108

22

opposite MATISSE:
The Young Sailor.
1906. See page 86

MATISSE:
Large Interior in Red.
1948. See page 104

opposite MUNCH:
The Voice.
1893. See page 76

FEININGER:
Alley of Trees.
1914. See page 164

GRIS: *Violin and Guitar.*
1913. See page 160

PICASSO:
Portrait of a Young Girl.
1914. See page 162

opposite KANDINSKY:
Little Pleasures.
1913. See page 120

CHAGALL: *Birthday.*
1915. See page 182

ROUSSEAU:
The Merry Jesters.
c. 1906. See page 176

opposite   BRAUNER:
Prelude to a Civilization.
1954. See page 200

PICASSO:
Women of Algiers.
1955. See page 258

IMPRESSIONISM

THE MODEL for this painting was Léon Koëlla-Leenhoff, who posed in Manet's studio on the Rue Guyot toward the end of 1861, when he was not quite ten years old. The date 1861 and a second signature, which had both been added around the beginning of this century, were removed in a recent cleaning. The long heavy sword is a seventeenth-century weapon that Manet borrowed for the picture from his friend the painter Charles Monginot, and the costume is of the same period. Léon, or Léon Edouard as he is named in the record of his birth, was born in 1852, the son of Suzanne Leenhoff, a Dutch pianist who eleven years later became Manet's wife. He was usually known as her youngest brother, but it has frequently been hinted that he was the natural child of Manet. As a young man he worked for a time as bank clerk under Auguste de Gas, the father of Edgar Degas the painter. He later became the proprietor of a successful firm that sold agricultural products.

In its decided contrasts of light and shadow the *Boy with a Sword* clearly shows the Spanish influence that is so marked in much of Manet's work during the first half of the sixties. Indeed the silhouette against the low horizon, the stance of the boy, and the diagonal of the sword vividly recall Jusepe de Ribera's painting of a club-footed boy that was in Paris in Manet's time and was given to the Louvre in 1869. Since Manet's painting had a fairly smooth surface and an agreeable and traditional subject not unusual during the second Empire, the public received it with less hostility than other works by Manet.

Margaretta M. Salinger

GIACOMO Meyerbeer's first French opera, *Robert le Diable*, which had been steadily performed since its premiere in 1831, provided Degas with the subject of this picture. Lillian Browse, who has made a careful study of the ballet in Degas's time, suggests that he was inspired by the production of 1871 in which Mme Laure Fonta led the ballet of the nuns. He chose the scene in which the spirits of the nuns, who have left their tombs by moonlight, circulate in the cloister. His unpublished notebooks include drawings for the composition and the following note about the setting: "In the recession of the arcades the moonlight barely touches the columns—on the ground the effect is rosier and warmer than I have made it. Vaults black, arches indefinite. The panel of footlights is reflected by the lamps. Tree much grayer. Luminous blue around the arches in perspective. The second version. Men more in color—flannelly but more vague. In the front the arches are grayer and darker. The black and in the vaulting in perspective . . . Slight reflection in the center." Degas's customary interest in the effects of light on forms and shapes was extended in this picture to the dramatic contrast between the brilliantly lit action on the stage and the less illuminated areas of the musicians' pit and the floor of the orchestra. This contrast had already been treated by the German artist Adolf Menzel in his *Théâtre du Gymnase*, painted in 1856, now in the National Gallery, Berlin, and also by Daumier in a lithograph of 1852 and in his painting *The Melodrama* of 1856–58, now in the Neue Staatsgalerie, Munich. Degas, a great admirer of the work of Daumier, must have known these two works, and he probably knew the Menzel, since he copied one of Menzel's pictures while the German artist was working in Paris and very likely studied others. Furthermore, Menzel's painting includes two motifs that appear in Degas's work: the neck of a double bass silhouetted against the footlights, as in the Metropolitan Museum's *Rehearsal of the Ballet on the Stage*, and spectators using their binoculars. In *The Ballet from "Robert le Diable,"* the painter's friend Désiré Dihau, the bassoonist, can be recognized, and beside him is another friend, Albert Hecht, with opera glasses.

Margaretta M. Salinger

DEGAS: *The Ballet from "Robert le Diable."* 1872.
Oil on canvas, 26 x 21⅜".
The Metropolitan Museum of Art,
New York. The H. O. Havemeyer
Collection.
Bequest of Mrs. H. O. Havemeyer

THIS PAINTING was done the year before Manet's death, when he was crippled by illness and confined to the garden of his country home. It is close in time to his last great painting, the *Bar at the Folies-Bergères* of 1882, in the Courtauld Institute, London. At the same time he was also painting small watercolors of flowers, fruit, and snails.

There are at least six paintings of the Rueil garden—large direct studies that demonstrate Manet's abbreviative manner of painting and the radical informality of his subject treatment. In other paintings of the garden Manet has shown even less of the house; the focus in all the views is on the variations of green in the garden. It is one of the traditional—and inaccurate—notions of Impressionism that colors are separated by the artist on the canvas and then blended by the eye. Manet's painting is a virtuoso piece in green and the variations of green. He has mixed his color on the palette: it is not a separation of blue and yellow, although intense blue haunts the shadows of the garden and yellow sits on the sunlit parts.

The contrasts of light that abound in this charming untended garden are aggressively set on dark tones to sharpen the sudden change of light. The grass and trees are studied principally for these changes, for the filtering through of sunshine and dark shadows. Bright flower colors among the green are not emphasized, for the green holds the key of interest. The focusing on a small piece of garden of uneven foliage, with the trunk of the tree placed without compromise almost in the middle of the canvas, is a casual and untraditional viewpoint which combines with Manet's swift, informal brush treatment. The painter has forsaken the frame of reference of horizon and sky to paint the grass at his feet. With Manet we move toward the attention to close patterns of earth that will become part of a new orientation in modern art.

Ursula Hoff and Margaret Plant

MANET: *House at Rueil.* 1882.
Oil on canvas, 36½ x 29".
National Gallery of Victoria,
Melbourne. Felton Bequest

RENOIR has organized this canvas in his usual fashion with a high horizon line. What is somewhat unusual is setting a block of space to occupy the entire foreground volume of the painting, one which is defined by the rustic wattle fence set parallel to the plane of the picture. The reality of this void is reinforced in its spaciousness by the placement of Monet's easel, his umbrella, his paint-box, and by the unusual solidity of his body and its position in the pictorial volume it emphasizes. This volume is further reinforced by the pattern of the foliage with its undulating edges on the ground in front of the fence.

The monumentality of the picture is further enhanced by the soaring hedge of variously colored roses in full bloom. The hedge itself has a volume which is meticulously suggested by the placement of the flowers. Beyond the rose hedge, a large open space is implied by the yellow-green hedge at the right of the canvas and by the soaring tree at the left corner of the picture. The solid form of the house beside the tree serves to enclose the whole picture volume at the left of the painting. At the right of the picture, the houses receding in parallel progression into space are neatly and precisely described, as if they had been rendered with the help of a camera obscura. The final emphasis upon spatial reality is achieved by the cloud patterns, which remind the viewer that the sky not only forms a background to the whole but also envelops the whole and projects to the very front and top edge of the painting, even as it describes an infinite distance.

Renoir has here equaled Pissarro at his best, and also Cézanne, in his insistence upon the reality of both the solid and the void, the reality of forms as they exist in space and as they are so seen. In this picture Renoir also has reacted to the reality and beauty not only of color but also of light and the interaction between these two natural phenomena.

John Maxon

RENOIR: *Monet Painting in His Garden*. c. 1874.

Oil on canvas, 18⅜ x 23½".
Wadsworth Atheneum, Hartford, Conn.
Bequest of Anne Parrish Titzell.
See color plate, page 18

VENICE seems a city reserved to pictures on postcards and to the paintings of Canaletto and Turner. However, two Impressionists, Renoir and Monet, also captured her as their own. Renoir visited Venice thirty years after Turner's death, Monet in 1908. Both painters were close friends and almost exact contemporaries. Once at the Louvre when they were young Monet had stopped before a painting by Canaletto and exclaimed: "Look, he does not even put in the reflections of the boats!"

In 1881 Renoir traveled to Italy. During the autumn, he visited Venice, Rome, Naples and Capri, Sicily, and Florence. He seems to have painted only in Venice and Naples and in Palermo, where Wagner (who had just completed *Parsifal*) consented to sit for a portrait—for half an hour.

This view, one also chosen by Turner (with Canaletto painting it!), is from San Giorgio Maggiore. Opposite the Campanile stands the Palazzo Ducale which is joined to the Prigioni by the Bridge of Sighs on which Byron's Childe Harold once stood, "a palace and a prison in each hand." To the left of the Campanile are the Library and the Zecca. In the distance can be seen San Marco mounted by its bronze horses and even a large fluttering flag, the green and white and red banner adopted by Napoleon and unfurled once again when Venice was unified with Italy in 1866.

During his visit, Renoir painted perhaps his most Impressionist picture, the lagoon veiled by fog. This sun-drenched picture is much more literal. The factual, indeed extremely detailed, architectural vista divides the sky, loosely painted in broad strokes, from the water, which is painted in a Divisionist technique with flecks of blue, red, yellow, green, purple and white. The entire surface sparkles with the dazzling radiance which had so fascinated Turner and, later, Monet. In Renoir's painting gondolas and yellow sails glide, almost at random, across the lagoon. Their movement seems curiously arrested; nevertheless they offer one of the endlessly changing aspects of the city.

In Monet's much later and more freely painted view, a close-up of the Doge's Palace (page 51), the gondolas are at rest. They nestle, sultry in shadow, as a slight but necessary diagonal between the shimmering, crenellated facade and its moist, mirror image. On his way back to Paris, Renoir visited Cézanne at L'Estaque (page 59). There he found a landscape more unchanging, where land and water do not seem to meet.

W.S.L.

RENOIR: *Venice, The Doge's Palace.* 1881.

Oil on canvas, 21⅜ x 25¾".
Sterling and Francine Clark
Art Institute, Williamstown, Mass.

NO OTHER landscape motif (except, perhaps, Cézanne's Mont Sainte-Victoire) has been subject to so close a scrutiny, has been the setting for such a range of subjective experience, or has been the source of so rich a harvest of art works as Monet's water garden. In 1890, after the purchase of the farmhouse in which he lived at Giverny, he acquired a tract of flood land that lay across the road and the one-track railroad from his front gateway. On it grew some poplars, and a tiny branch of the Epte River provided a natural boundary.

Excavation was immediately begun to result, after several enlargements of the plan, in a 100 by 300 foot pond through which the flow of water from the river was controlled by a sluice at either end. Curvilinear and organic in shape, it narrowed at the western end to pass beneath a Japanese footbridge. Willows, bamboo, lilies, iris, rose arbors, benches, and on one shore curving steps leading to the water were added, providing a luxuriant setting for the spectacle of cloud reflections and water lilies floating on the pond's surface. Except for a single gate, the water garden was fenced with wire upon which rambling roses were entwined; sealed off from the outside world it formed an encircling whole; a work of art with nature as its medium, conceived not as a painting subject, but as a retreat for delectation and meditation.

The twenty-seven-year period of water landscapes begins with the series of the Japanese footbridge exhibited at the Durand-Ruel Gallery in Paris in 1900 and in New York a few months later. It was on this bridge that Monet stood to meditate and watch the lily blossoms open in the forenoon and close late in the day.

The first impact of these works is of an almost tropical profusion of trees, shrubs, festoons of weeping willow, and iris beds; its exotic abundance, dramatized by florid accents, is akin to the extravagant literary descriptions of Monet's fiend Octave Mirbeau or the atonal music of Debussy and Stravinsky. Upon the saturated greens, blues, siennas, and ochers of the pool and its wavering reflections, the lily pads and blossoms, viewed in recession, lie like a rich but tattered carpet worked with threads of pink and white.

William C. Seitz

MONET: *Water Lilies and Japanese Bridge.* 1899.

Oil on canvas, 35⅝ x 35⅜".
The Art Museum, Princeton University, Princeton.
From the Collection of William Church Osborn, Class of 1883, Trustee of Princeton University (1914–51), President of The Metropolitan Museum of Art (1941–47). Given by His Family

IN THE OPEN water Monet's gardeners were kept busy pruning groups of lily pads into circular units. Searching among them his eyes found arrangements that gradually began to exclude the shore entirely. By 1903 a new relationship of space and flatness had evolved. Its patterns are open, curvilinear, and expanding, and of a random naturalness; yet the clusters are nevertheless held in mutual attraction by a geometry as nebulous as that of the clouds whose reflections passed over the pond's surface. It is surprising how little "aesthetic distance" separates these images from photographic actuality; yet in their isolation from other things, and because of the mood they elicit, they seem, like pure thought or meditation, abstract.

It is an ironic reminder of the artist's predicament that Monet found as much anguish in struggling to represent his garden as he did satisfaction in contemplating it. In August 1908, after ten years during which he painted it each summer, he wrote to Gustave Geffroy that "these landscapes of water and reflections have become an obsession. They are beyond the powers of an old man, and I nevertheless want to succeed in rendering what I perceive. I destroy them . . . I recommence them . . . and I hope that from so many efforts, something will come out."

After he returned from his first Venice trip in 1908, Monet saw his canvases of the water garden with a "better eye," and began choosing from them for an exhibition to be called *Les Nymphéas: Série de Paysages d'Eau.* Forty-eight, dated between 1903 and 1908, were shown in May 1909 at Durand-Ruel's. The conception of an ovoid salon decorated with water landscapes probably entered Monet's mind (if he had not thought of it earlier) at this time. It was apparent that the individual canvases of water lilies, though carefully composed and therefore satisfying in themselves, were also fragments that begged to be brought together in an encompassing whole.

William C. Seitz

MONET: *Water Lilies.* 1907.

Oil on canvas, 35½ x 28½".
Lydia and Harry Lewis Winston
Collection (Dr. and Mrs.
Barnett Malbin, New York)

DISCOURAGED, troubled with weakening eyesight, attacks of vertigo, and fatigue, in September of 1908 Monet accepted an invitation to visit Venice, where he had never been. He was delighted with Venice, and regretted not having visited it earlier; but even though he extended his stay until December and returned again the following fall, most of the pictures were completed at Giverny. After many interruptions, twenty-nine canvases representing nine motifs were shown at the Bernheim-Jeune Gallery in 1912. Except for a romantic view of San Giorgio Maggiore at twilight, they share a common, generalized interpretation of the rose, blue, and violet tremolo of Venetian light. Because they were finished from memory, Monet felt that nature had "had its revenge," and he was deeply dissatisfied. "I know very well in advance that you will find my canvases perfect," he wrote to Durand-Ruel before the exhibition, ". . . that they will have great success, but that makes no difference to me since I know they are bad and am certain of it."

Of this buoyantly beautiful group of paintings, the close-up views of palaces are especially interesting. Ignoring romantic clichés, and advancing from the precedent of his series of *Poplars* and the *Rouen Cathedrals*, Monet affixed the truncated facade to the tops of his composition, square with the frame and exactly parallel to the canvas surface. The rhythmic horizontal and vertical architectural divisions reinforce the sparkle of light and shadow on the lapping water. In place of hackneyed *bizarrerie*, Monet has given us an urbane formal structure; the active upper portion pushes forward, while the horizontal water surface fades into the building's vertical reflection.

These paintings of Venice are the last of Monet's architectural works and the purest examples of the levitational predisposition that ties his art to that of the twentieth century. "It seems that the rose and blue facades float on the water," wrote a young French writer, Henri Genet, when the pictures were exhibited.

William C. Seitz

MONET: *Venice,*
The Doge's Palace. 1908.

Oil on canvas, 32 x 39⅝".
The Brooklyn Museum.
Gift of A. Augustus Healy

ALTHOUGH several brilliant and elaborate flower paintings date from Monet's early years, still lifes are rarely found in his later work, where he devoted himself almost exclusively to the study of the transitory effects of light and atmosphere on outdoor subjects, notably in the series representing the exotic luxuriance of his garden at Giverny (pages 47, 49).

This opalescent late still life, an overall pink-lilac-violet in color, is exceptional in Monet's expressive work of the period. For here we find comparative clarity of outline, formal definition, symmetry, and a static realization of subject matter, enveloped in even, pervasive light. Furthermore, it is a traditional representation (recalling Chardin), a rare occurrence with Monet, who had little interest in the old masters.

Finally, one may boldly suggest that its composition owes something to Cézanne, Monet's contemporary and friend, with whom he had, aesthetically, parted company many years previously. In any event, its formality challenges the critic Roger Fry's lack of sympathy with Monet's scientific and sensuous documentation of appearances. Fry considered the *Water Lilies* series "shockingly organized, so totally without a proper compositional skeleton." Then Fry, an honest man and not totally hidebound by theory, would add, characteristically, "And yet . . . and yet."

Such strictures delivered by the champion of "plastic values" and "significant form" cannot fairly be applied to this still life. But however classical in spirit it may be, Monet could not help approaching form in his own way. Shapes exist clearly enough yet, being bathed in semi-abstract color luminosity, all but lose individual, local color. The result is extremely beautiful in a dreamlike fashion without relapsing into trancelike vagueness. The painting embodies Monet's principles and practice at their calmest, their most delicate and visionary.

Stuart Preston

MONET: *Still Life with a Basket of Eggs.* c. 1910.
Oil on canvas, 29⅜ x 36⅞".
Collection Mrs. Lloyd Bruce Wescott, Rosemont, N.J.
See color plate, page 19

POST-IMPRESSIONISM

IN 1877, when he painted this portrait of his wife, Cézanne was in full possession of his peculiar genius; he saw his goal ahead, saw it steadily, and saw it whole. It is best summed up in his own words: "I have not tried to reproduce nature; I have represented her." Left far behind him were the wildly romantic paintings of his youth, to which his temperament was utterly unsuited. And behind him, too, the Impressionists' purely visual grasp of things seen, although they, particularly Pissarro, had taught him much in the way of lightening his palette and demonstrating that the world about him— landscapes, figures, still lifes—offered material for infinite enrichment. But, not for him the sensuousness of Renoir or the lyricism of Monet. A true classic, he missed in Impressionism nature's permanence and structural design, ignored in the capturing of purely transitory images.

Cézanne's aim, as he declared, was "to make of Impressionism something solid and lasting, like the art of museums." "Our art," he told a friend, "should give to nature the thrill of continuance with the appearance of all its changes. It should enable us to feel nature as eternal." Hence the elimination of all that he considered inessential in "realizing" (his own word) enduring reality.

In truth, his wife is portrayed not so much as the Provençale bourgeoise that she was but as a veritable Rock of Ages. Roger Fry, one of Cézanne's earliest and most eloquent champions, wrote that this portrait expresses "that characteristic feeling of Cézanne's —perhaps at its intensest at this period—of the monumental repose, the immense duration of the objects represented." And, again to quote Cézanne: "When color has its richness form has its plenitude." Subtlety of color here is complicated and profound, creating a sturdy, mosaiclike harmony made up of the olive yellow, blue-starred wallpaper, the reddish armchair ("in itself a personage," observed Rilke), the varied blues of the bodice, and the lighter and darker greens of the striped skirt. And how wonderfully all these discrete elements have been locked together, formally and chromatically. Nothing has been left to chance.

The composition fills the whole picture space, every small or large incident depending on its neighbor. Cézanne here reconciles visual facts with the kind of hieratic pictorial organization at which he excelled. Yet the final impression made by this monolithic portrait is not an inhuman one. Far from it.

Stuart Preston

CEZANNE: *Mme Cézanne in a Red Armchair.* c. 1877.

Oil on canvas, 28½ x 22".
Museum of Fine Arts, Boston.
The Robert Treat Paine, 2nd Bequest

ANYONE visiting Provence, Cézanne's native countryside, will at once realize how profoundly that artist made it his own—to such a degree, in fact, that we see it mainly through his eyes. Wisely, later artists have largely avoided depicting his favorite "motifs," those fragments of nature which he virtually copyrighted. To make a new pictorial assault on Mont Sainte-Victoire would amount to an act of lèse-majesté.

The same observations can be made about Cézanne's numerous paintings of L'Estaque, a small fishing port on the Bay of Marseilles, where he lived on and off between the 1870s and the 1890s. He deeply attached his vision to this harsh, arid, and yet mysterious landscape, where a relentlessly blazing sun makes vivid contrasts between the somber greens of the twisted pine and olive trees, the white of bleached rocks, and the flat blue of the sea with its limitless horizon.

This picture (once owned by Monet) is one of Cézanne's finest and largest versions of the L'Estaque motif, in which he focuses his marvelous perceptive powers and his selective fidelity on visual sensations and evokes a feeling of monumental timelessness. Indeed, time seems to have come to a stop. This is a corner of the Mediterranean world, past, present, and future. Rocks and trees and open sea seem to be bound together by some powerful eternal relationship which connects all the interweaving shapes, large and small. The miracle is his ability to render deep space without using the Impressionist method of aerial perspective. This he accomplished by splitting up form into facets of mosaiclike color which subtly lead the eye from foreground to background. The complicated procedure required Cézanne's genius to control the many diverse elements so that they lock together into a lucid, overall design.

Stuart Preston

CEZANNE: *L'Estaque.* 1882-85.
Oil on canvas, 31½ x 39".
The Museum of Modern Art,
New York. Gift of
William S. Paley, the donor
retaining life interest

THESE TWO paintings of bathers by a river belong to a series of works which Cézanne painted from the early 1870s until his death in 1906. They are curiously enigmatic. There are no clear relationships between the figures whose poses are tense and unstable, whose expressions are either anguished or blank, and whose gestures are strong but motiveless. Moreover, in these paintings Cézanne contradicted the fundamental principle of painting from nature which guided all the other works of his maturity. These *Bathers* were collections of single figures drawn from an extraordinary range of sources and pieced together like interchangeable parts. This can be seen, for instance, in the way the striding figure is repeated with only slight variations, and in the inconsistencies of scale in the later male *Bathers*.

Given the subject—the traditional idyll of harmony between man and nature—it is strange that many of the figures were drawn from works which represent physical or sexual violence, anguish or death, and that their inherent strain is intensified by the structure of the paintings. For example, as the steep bank in the earlier female *Bathers* gives the ample figures no space in which to exist, they seem about to slide forward out of the painting. In this sense, there is little to choose between the two paintings, although they were painted nearly twenty years apart and although, in the same period, Cézanne moved from rather tight, almost schematic to superbly spacious and harmonious landscapes, still lifes, and portraits. Cézanne's series of *Bathers*, on the other hand, show him almost obsessively repeating a limited number of images which obviously had some profound inner meaning.

The meaning clearly lay in his personal life—in his desire for, and fear of, women; in his own illegitimate birth; his liaison with a woman who bore him a son whose existence Cézanne hid from his deeply feared father for more than fifteen years; his memories of the days when he and his childhood friend Emile Zola roamed the Provencal countryside, bathed in rivers, recited poetry, planned their future as great artists and talked of their voluptuous dreams of women—so that dreams of the enjoyment and terror of sex were fused with dreams of art and with memories of sensual abandon to nature.

In the early 1870s Cézanne was influenced by Impressionist paintings of picnics in the country, but whereas they represented happy, easy relationships between the sexes, he expressed extreme sexual tension (seen more overtly in his contemporary paintings of rape and murder). However, when he underwent the extraordinary discipline to the Impressionist ideal of truth to nature, he also began to abandon such scenes. When he depicted figures in nature, he tended to separate the sexes and to discipline his previous romantic violence with a strong geometric framework (as in the

CEZANNE: *Bathers*. 1882–85.
Oil on canvas, 15 x 18".
Private collection, Switzerland

60

earlier female *Bathers*). This development suggests an intimate connection between Cézanne's dedication to nature and to the seeking out of an internally coherent structure with which to embody his "sensation" and his need to control his sexual imagination.

It is this blend of passion and detachment which makes these paintings so moving: they confront us with something which is extraordinarily intimate (which, like any profound confession, becomes more enigmatic as it is more revealing), and they lead one to consider the nature of the man's need to create form. Few paintings, indeed, reveal themselves so nakedly. For example, in the male *Bathers* Cézanne sought the forms of the figures with tenuous nervous lines which he repeated again and again so that one is made aware of the very process by which he created form. The blue lines which are associated with the bodies are no different in kind from the lines of the branches, and they thus reveal something of the way the painter establishes a sense of wholeness and makes sense from the randomness of experience. The hesitant lines and delicate strokes of color show how Cézanne felt his way to his forms and made manifest his passionate desire to make those forms—whether those of nature or of his emotion—real for himself through painting.

Virginia Spate

CEZANNE: *Bathers.*
c. 1895–1900.

Oil on canvas, 10⅝ x 18⅛".
The Baltimore Museum of Art.
Cone Collection

THIS WORK is a major figure by Cézanne. One hesitates to say portrait, for by the time that this work was painted, Cézanne had but the slightest interest in likenesses as such, if indeed he ever did. What the painter does here, with the aid of his patient wife and kindest sitter, is to give the viewer a concentrated image of a personage seated and composed in a chair. This personage is painted in such a way as to suggest the greatest mass and, with the concomitant result, the impression that the subject might just as well be made of painted stone as of flesh and bone. Cézanne has subjected his wife to the same intense and analytical scrutiny which he used for plates of apples, the Montagne Sainte-Victoire, or the avenue of chestnut trees in his garden at the Jas de Bouffan.

Cézanne's accomplishment in such a work as this great picture is to re-create in his own terms the whole art of figure painting. These terms were, of course, the adjustment of the drawing employed to the exigencies of the overall pictorial structure in both two and three dimensions, and the adjustment of the paint strokes so as to describe not only the effect of light on objects but to relate these patches as they were portrayed to the same overall pictorial structure. The method was infinitely laborious, and in Cézanne's occasional failures merely labored. In this monumental work, the slow, even tedious method has produced an intensely felt and observed image.

John Maxon

CEZANNE: *Mme Cézanne in a Yellow Chair.* 1893-95.

Oil on canvas, 31⅞ x 25½".
The Art Institute of Chicago.
Wilson L. Mead Fund.
See color plate, page 20.

THOUGH HE died only in 1949, James Ensor, the foremost Belgian painter since the time of Rubens, was born four years before Toulouse-Lautrec and only a year later than Seurat. Like Redon he worked at first in a realistic style, but during the 1880s he and Redon took their places at the extreme left of the modern movement as the two great masters of imaginative freedom.

Ensor lived all his very long life at Ostend, but by 1887, when he painted the *Fireworks* and the *Tribulation of St. Anthony*, in The Museum of Modern Art, he was already familiar with the work of the Paris vanguard through the annual exhibitions of the Brussels Société des XX, then the most progressive art society in the world.

Ensor went beyond the Impressionists and flatly rejected the scientifically rational theory and technique of Seurat's Neo-Impressionism, which was then the last word in Paris. He was half-English and probably knew J. M. W. Turner's luminous reds and yellows and bold handling of light. As in the *St. Anthony*, he uses any color he pleases, and his brush swirls and slashes over his canvas with a freedom which matches the audacity of his imagination. Indeed, at this moment in his career, Ensor was possibly the boldest living painter. Gauguin was still painting semi-Impressionist pictures, and only in the following year, 1888, was van Gogh, under the burning sun of Arles, able to free himself from Impressionism. Ensor's *St. Anthony* of 1887 points the way not only toward the unfettered humor and fantasy of Klee and the Surrealists Miró, Max Ernst, and André Masson, but also toward the abstract expressionism of Kandinsky and his descendants among the younger artists of the mid-twentieth century.

Alfred H. Barr, Jr.

AMONG THE paintings of the later 1880s, a brilliant period in Ensor's production, the solid painterly accomplishments which so many of the earlier drawings prepared for were joined with Ensor's unique imagination. The *Fireworks* of 1887 is an outstanding example of the real and imaginary combined in an unforgettable vision. The conception of the picture in itself is exceptional. In a vast landscape, many small figures stroll as in a large park. Rendered with sure touches, like the figures in the backgrounds of Manet's paintings, they establish the scale of the picture. Over the low dark horizon bursts an enormous display of incandescent yellow and orange fireworks, placed against a sky divided into intense bands of blue and red. The size of the explosion is so great as to suggest some unimaginable cataclysm, yet the foreground strollers promenade as though nothing unusual was happening. This ambiguity is characteristic of Ensor's work; even where his representations are filled with detail a sense of enigma prevails.

Dennis Adrian

ENSOR: *Fireworks*. 1887.
Oil and encaustic on canvas, 40¼ x 44½
Albright-Knox Art Gallery,
Buffalo.
George B. and Jenny R. Mathews Fund

SIGNAC had painted at Port-en-Bessin in 1882 and 1883, and it was he who suggested the site to Seurat when they met in 1884. The latter painted six canvases there in 1888, in rapid succession.

In this view, the sea has receded and with it its assault against dry land has been temporarily removed. In front of the stone breakwater and the houses a slimy tidal flat has been exposed. Though full of life, this is the sea in its least impressive aspect.

What is given here is another of those great silences Seurat was so good at expressing in his landscapes. It communicates tranquillity and fills the viewer with a kind of contentment. The absence of people has something to do with this.

Port-en-Bessin is built up in horizontal layers—the sea wall, the breakwaters, the horizon line, the sky. It is a delicate work, more nearly suggested than stated, perhaps even a bit understated, but the colors and tonalities have persuasive charm. With his Pointillist technique (even the signature is "beaded"), Seurat succeeds in giving universality to his subject, objectifying it enough so that we forget, not the name of the place (he was anxious to remind us of it), but any too narrowly regional associations. The work might as aptly, or perhaps even more aptly, be titled "Low Tide."

Pierre Courthion

SEURAT: *Port-en-Bessin: The Outer Harbor.* 1888.
Oil on canvas, 21¼ x 25¾".
The St. Louis Art Museum

SEURAT shared Cézanne's desire "to make of Impressionism something durable." In this endeavor, he was the first modern painter to apply scientific theory to his work in a systematic, rigorous way. His color research had been influenced by the works of the great colorists of the past, especially Delacroix, but even more by the recent scientific research in the fields of physics and optics, particularly the principle of "simultaneous contrast of colors" formulated by M. E. Chevreul in 1839.

With tiny brushstrokes in the form of dots, Seurat proceeded by first laying down the local color of the object and then "achromatizing" it by adding colors corresponding to reflected and absorbed light and to surrounding objects and complementary atmospheric effects. The colors were laid down in pure unmixed form, blending optically in the observer's eye.

Repercussions of Seurat's method and theories were felt for generations to come. They directly influenced the brilliant color harmonies of several painters in this exhibition: Delaunay, Kupka, Derain, and Picasso.

Susana Leval

FOR SEVERAL years Signac had painted Impressionist landscapes with strong colors and impetuous brushwork. In the months just before the last Impressionist exhibition of May 1886, he adopted Seurat's more rigorous technique and color theory in paintings like this one, shown in the May exhibition. The center of the picture is dominated by the opposition of orange-red and blue, but the sky and foreground have little in the way of contrasts, and the brushstroke retains considerable softness and variety.

Vincent van Gogh was much impressed by Signac when they met, and he may have been inspired by this picture or one like it when he painted his own view of factories seen across a meadow, a picture once in the collection of Père Tanguy, whom Signac had known already in 1883. Signac's social consciousness was vested in his lifelong adherence to Anarchist-Communism, a parallel to van Gogh's religious convictions. Industrial subjects appropriate to such views were frequent in his work in the mid-1880s, as they were in the paintings of Albert Dubois-Pillet, Charles Angrand, Maximilien Luce, and Lucien Pissarro at exactly the same time, and in the drawings of Seurat. In their concern for modern urban life, the Neo-Impressionists and their friends among the Symbolists found a point of contrast with the older Impressionists, whom they regarded as middle-class conservatives.

This painting has sometimes been confused with a very similar one of the same date, *Passage du Puits Bertin* (in a private collection in England), partly because Félix Fénéon inverted the titles of the two in his review of the 1886 exhibition.

Robert L. Herbert

SIGNAC: *Gas Tanks at Clichy.* 1886.

Oil on canvas, 25½ x 31⅞". National Gallery of Victoria, Melbourne. Felton Bequest

VAN GOGH has been the subject of unrelenting research. In addition, the drama of his life embellishes as well as obscures the appreciation of his art. He himself remains his best biographer, and his letters, chiefly to his brother, Theo, offer an inexhaustible source of information.

Van Gogh's maturity as an artist spans scarcely a decade. At the beginning of 1886 he arrived in Paris. During the next two years, the second and final development of his style as a painter was rapid. The vigor and power of his earlier paintings in Holland was not lost. But their sometimes heavy realism was muted by a more selective observation and, eventually, would be eclipsed by a lyric animism seldom as eloquently achieved by any painter.

Van Gogh struggled with Impressionism and with Seurat's Pointillist method. In 1887 he also studied intensely a few Japanese color woodcuts, by various artists, which had been printed earlier in the nineteenth century. These confirmed foreshortenings and close-ups he had already used, with instinctive authority, in the composition of earlier drawings and paintings in Holland.

In 1888, van Gogh was thirty-five years old. In February he left Paris for the south of France. In the short period until his death in May 1890, he was prolific, producing more than fifteen hundred drawings and almost half as many paintings.

Among these works are the magnificent drawings in reed pen and ink for which he is best known as a craftsman. Further study of Japanese prints had led him to illustrations by Hokusai. These prints were actually engravings of drawings which, in stark contrasts of black and white, combined stippled areas with animated flowing curves.

Van Gogh quickly mastered the reed pen as an instrument of drawing. He used it as a brush and as a scribe, alternating its rhythms and fluctuations. Swirls, dots, and strokes burst with energy across the sheet of paper. The drawings usually relate to specific paintings, as does the view of the small fishing village Saintes-Maries (page 12). The painting, unfortunately, has been lost.

Such drawings influenced van Gogh's technique of painting. For instance, in this view of a corridor in Saint Paul's Hospital in Saint Rémy (an asylum), the influence of reed-pen drawing is apparent in the broken lines which define the paving of the passage and which indicate the curves of the vaulted ceiling.

W.S.L.

VAN GOGH:
Hospital Corridor. 1889.
Gouache and watercolor
on paper, 24⅛ x 18⅝".
The Museum of Modern Art,
New York.
Abby Aldrich Rockefeller Bequest

72

GAUGUIN'S *Man with an Axe* was painted in Tahiti shortly after his arrival in June 1891. Finding Papeete too Europeanized, he settled in the district of Mataiea, thirty miles away. After a few difficult, lonely weeks, he slowly began to make contact with the natives and to learn their language. Soon he began to work furiously, dazzled by the native colors and landscape.

Man with an Axe represents a scene Gauguin watched one day from his hut and later described in *Noa Noa*, his early Tahitian memoirs: "It is morning. On the sea, by the shore, I see a pirogue and in the pirogue a woman. On the shore a man almost naked . . . With a harmonious and subtle gesture the man raises with his two hands a heavy axe which leaves a blue mark against the silvery sky, and—below—its incision on the dead tree . . . On the purple soil, long serpentine leaves of a metallic yellow seemed to me like the written characters of a faraway Oriental language . . . In the pirogue a woman was arranging some nets. The blue line of the sea was frequently broken by the green crests of the rolling surf crashing against the coral reefs."

In *Man with an Axe* Gauguin transformed a specific visual experience into an extraordinarily beautiful painting. The vibrant, saturated colors, freed from what he called the "timidity of expression of degenerate races," were chosen not for their descriptive value, but for their pictorial expressiveness. Gauguin previously had asserted the painter's right to create a pictorial world independent of the real world and based solely on aesthetic considerations. "How do you see those trees?" he demanded of the young painter Paul Sérusier, in 1888. "They are yellow. Well, then, put down yellow. And that shadow is rather blue. So render it with pure ultramarine. Those red leaves? Use vermilion." These new principles formed the basis of Gauguin's unquestioned leadership in the modern movement.

The composition, too, has been ordered so as to yield its highest pictorial, rather than representational, value. The entire vista from shore to horizon has been radically compressed into a single plane of waving, luminous bands. The uncompromising flatness is enhanced by the sensuous linear patterns, culminating in the sinuous forms at the lower left corner, curious premonitions of the Art Nouveau style. The pose of the man in this picture reappears in identical fashion a year later in *Matamoe*; that of the bending woman, in *Tahitian Fisherwomen* of 1891.

Susana Leval

GAUGUIN: *Man with an Axe.*
1891.

Oil on canvas, 36¼ x 27¼".
Collection Mr. and Mrs. Alex M. Lewyt,
New York

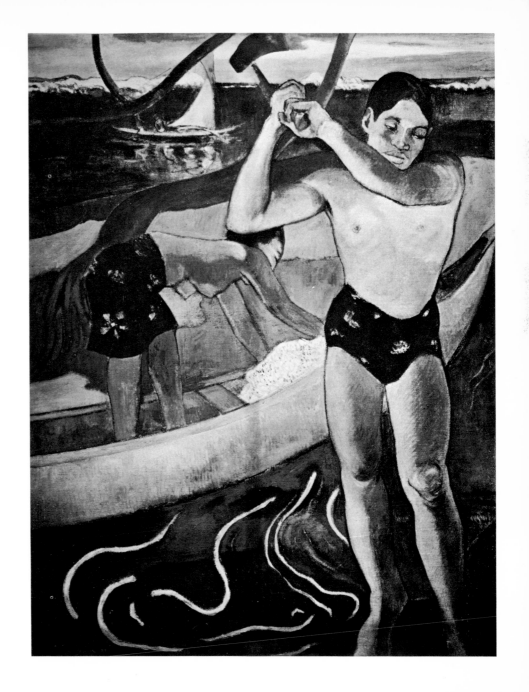

IT IS DIFFICULT to place the solitary figure of Edvard Munch in any summary of modern art. The foremost artist Scandinavia has produced, he was a contemporary of the Post-Impressionists in France and the senior of Bonnard and Vuillard, but he worked far into the twentieth century and died in 1944. Also, more than any other single artist, he is the father of Expressionism in Germany.

The fact that Munch's work is literary needs no defense. More interested in content than in the solution of aesthetic problems, he possessed an imagination fevered by deep personal reactions to the world around him. He has been compared to Redon in France and Ensor in Belgium. But Redon's visions were dreams, not nightmares, and the grotesque fantasy of Ensor remains essentially Flemish. Munch's revelations were cultivated by passion, with terror and, perhaps like Baudelaire's, with delight. "I paint not what I see, but what I saw," Munch wrote. "The camera cannot compete with painting since it cannot be used in Heaven or Hell."

The essential relationship of woman to man is the central theme in Munch's paintings and prints until 1908, when a fear of insanity, which had harassed him for years, became a reality. The theme is insistent, brooding, often brutal and erotic. Munch's attitude was described by his friend the playwright August Strindberg: "Man gives, creating the illusion that woman gives in return. Man begs the favor of giving his soul, his blood, his liberty, his repose, his eternal salvation, in exchange for what? In exchange for the happiness of giving his soul, his blood, his liberty, his repose, his eternal salvation."

The Voice, one of Munch's most beautifully colored compositions, was painted in Berlin in 1893. It seems, at first glance, the least troubled of his masterworks. A woman appears, surrounded by pine trees. Her dress shimmers, her face is cast by shadow. As so often with Munch, the standing figure is still but anxious. The straight, bare trunks emphasize her stance and situate her within the grove. Behind, in steep perspective, lie a beach and a fiord. The moon, a frequent apparition in the works of Munch, rises above its own reflection like the dot upon an "i." In the distance, an open boat with two passengers glides across the water.

The Voice, also called *Summer Night* and *Evening*, might in addition be entitled "The Assignation." The woman has kept an appointment with a man who has not yet appeared. The ithyphallic reflection, however, suggests his emotional if not physical presence. She waits expectant and, perhaps, menacing.

W.S.L.

MUNCH: *The Voice.* 1893.
Oil on canvas, 34½ x 42½".
Museum of Fine Arts, Boston.
Ernest Wadsworth Longfellow Fund.
See color plate, page 24

DESCENDED FROM the Dutch "little" masters and from Chardin, the French school of Intimism, one development of Impressionism, flourished during the 1890s. Painters found inspiration in the expression of tenderness toward the things they knew best, things which were part of the rhythm of their very daily existence. The style reached its most delicate flowering in the work of Vuillard.

This small painting depicts the Vuillard family—his grandmother, mother, sister, and brother-in-law (the painter K.-X. Roussel) at lunch in their apartment just off the Rue Saint-Honoré. Vuillard usually developed pictures such as this from summary sketches. "Many of them," wrote Jacques Salomon, "are simply brief notations . . . He would immediately proceed to paint . . . and his astonishing memory would bring back to him the color relations which it has registered."

The composition lacks the formality of a conversation piece. Resemblances are hinted rather than explicitly portrayed. The group almost melts into the background. The decorative elements, the wallpaper, the costumes, and the still life on the dinner table are visual delights. The composition is both subtle and bold; the influences of Japanese prints and, perhaps, photography account for the unexpected main motif— his sister's back and the chair on which she sits. Other elements fall into half-shadow.

Vuillard's domestic scenes distill feelings of family happiness. They tell us, in a minor and elusive fashion, much about human life. It is the presence of heart and soul and reason that constitutes half of Vuillard's charm. These qualities, united here, raise a banal subject far above the common and the conventional. Vuillard never descends to sentimentality or anecdote. Whatever his emotions about his sisters, he corrects feeling by a kind of detached, sometimes ironic objectivity. He was, as the painter Jacques-Emile Blanche remarked, "a gourmand turned ascetic."

The young Matisse noticed and profited from Intimist work by Vuillard and Bonnard. Their influence is still evident in Matisse's *Checker Game and Piano Music* (page 101), painted as late as 1923. "The three [artists] had a good deal in common," wrote Alfred Barr. "All were realists in the broadest sense of the word. They made paintings of what they saw in the world around them, in the studio, in rooms where people lived."

Stuart Preston

VUILLARD:
Family at Table. c. 1897.
Oil on board, 19½ x 28".
Private collection, New York

"HOW MANY DAYS have I spent alone with my cat," Bonnard once wrote, "and when I say *alone*, I mean without a material being, for my cat is a mystical companion, a spirit. . . ." Like that dachshund who appears so beguilingly and unexpectedly in many of his later pictures, the cat is one of the most enlivening images he ever summoned up, genielike, from his domestic surroundings—no mere tame pussy but an almost disturbing presence, perhaps symbolizing light, which vividly animates this otherwise solemn portrayal of a woman (almost certainly Mme Bonnard). Painted in 1912, this portrait exemplifies Bonnard's creative powers at their most original and appealing.

Bonnard used often mistakenly to be considered no more than a belated, if sensitive, Impressionist. It is true that Monet, whom he knew and admired, did influence him in as much as an artist of such independent talent could be influenced. However, he was not taken too seriously during the years when all highbrow attention was being stirred up by the successive aesthetic revolutions of Fauvism, Cubism, Dada, and Surrealism. They affected Bonnard not at all. So, from about 1910 to 1930, the pontiffs of modern art looked askance at the absence in his mysteriously radiant work of cubes, cylinders, mathematical equations, elements dredged out of Jung's collective unconscious, and other fashionable abstract fetishes of the period.

Not all critics missed the peculiar distinction of Bonnard's work. Painters particularly appreciated his refulgent color which, delicately applied, becomes a luminous substance in itself. The perceptive Jacques-Emile Blanche observed that Bonnard's color seemed to capture the quasi-mystical effect of sunlight streaming through stained-glass windows, a secular grace abounding.

And as for his strangely personal sense of design, which in this painting tends to diminish the third dimension, Clive Bell has this to say: "There is something Chinese about him [Bonnard]; and he is one of those rare Europeans who have dealt in 'imposed' rather than 'built-up' design. Bonnard's pictures as a rule grow not as trees; they float as water lilies. European pictures, as a rule, spring upward, masonry-wise, from their foundations; the design of a picture by Bonnard, like that of many Chinese pictures and Persian textiles, seems to have been laid on the canvas as one might lay cautiously on dry grass some infinitely precious figured gauze."

Stuart Preston

BONNARD: A *Woman with a Cat.* 1912.

Oil on canvas, 30¾ x 30¼".
Musée National d'Art Moderne, Paris.
The Baroness Napoléon Gourgaud
Bequest

MATISSE

MATISSE, surely, is the greatest colorist of our time. However, this small picture, with its contrasts of textured fabrics and of light and shade, still relates to the intimate interiors with figures by Vuillard and was painted contemporaneously with them. It is the earliest work by Matisse in the exhibition. The subject appears to be a Spanish guitar player. Actually, she is Mme Matisse, his devoted wife. To support their family she had opened a small millinery shop on the Rue de Chateaudun. In addition, because hiring models was expensive, she posed for many of her husband's early paintings.

Matisse's *Guitarist* invites deliberate comparison with Manet's *The Spanish Singer* or, to use Théophile Gautier's title, *The Guitarist*, painted in 1860 and now in the Metropolitan Museum of Art in New York. The painting has similar contrasts of light and dark, but Matisse probably knew better Manet's etching which repeats the subject and reverses the composition. The plate was etched in 1861, the year the painting was admired at the Salon. It was subsequently printed in several editions, and most likely Matisse owned a proof, as did Degas.

Years later, Matisse recalled an incident in the painting of the picture. It reveals something of the strain under which he and his wife lived and worked, a strain increased by financial burden. "My wife was posing for me in a dark blue toreador costume embroidered in silver. Her toe rested on a little stool in order to support the knee on which the guitar was resting. This position, which is not very comfortable for anyone who is not a guitar player, gave her cramps in her leg which, added to the long periods of absolute immobility required for posing, caused her to grow impatient. I, on the other hand, was absorbed in my work, quite silent and often intense as a result of the effort I was making. Suddenly my wife gave a quick pluck at the strings: ding, ding. I let this pass without comment. After it had happened several times, I realized that it was getting on my nerves. I told her so with all the gentleness of a person who is holding on to himself. Finally, when my wife repeated the same sign of exasperation as a sort of unconscious form of relaxation, I gave a vigorous kick against the bar of my easel which was oblique and very light-weight. The bar broke in two with a loud noise, the easel fell down as did also the canvas and oil cup which splattered everything. At this moment my wife threw the guitar on top of the other things with a gesture that was as quick as what had gone before. The guitar did not break, but we burst out laughing. This relaxed our nerves and united us in our gaiety as we had been united in our tension."

W.S.L.

MATISSE: *The Guitarist.* 1903.
Oil on canvas, 22 x 15⅜".
Collection Mr. and Mrs.
Ralph F. Colin, New York

THE TWO versions of *The Young Sailor* done at Collioure in 1906, it is said within the same month, reveal how Matisse transformed Fauve color and a rather heavy-handed study of structure into a composition of great decorative elegance. The first version, purchased by Michael and Sarah Stein, is rather somber in effect; the drawing is bold and rather angular; the hands and face are modeled in reddish lights and green shadows, the blouse is irregularly hatched in dull blue, the trousers in greens; the background is mottled and sketchy.

In the second version of *The Young Sailor*, shown here, the drawing of both outer silhouette and interior lines has become graceful and flowing. The luminous blue and green areas of the costume curve against a vermilion chair and solid pink background. The strong, sullen face of the first version is redrawn in bright green and pink lines to give an expression of almond-eyed charm verging on prettiness. The whole effect is supremely decorative. In fact *The Young Sailor* is perhaps the only other picture of 1906 that obviously appears to be by the painter of the *Joy of Life*, finished at the beginning of the year and now in the Barnes Foundation in Merion, Pennsylvania. But whereas the larger canvas seems labored and inconsistent in style, *The Young Sailor* is brought off with consummate ease and confidence. The Oriental influence in the *Joy of Life* seems comparatively unassimilated and artificial, as if assembled from a museum. *The Young Sailor* is of course a far simpler problem than the *Joy of Life*, but its Orientalism, though artful, is integrated. Its technique is as deft, its color as fresh and translucent as that of the folk craftsmen who decorated the pottery and tiles and plastered walls of Biskra, which Matisse had admired on his visit there a very short time before.

Alfred H. Barr, Jr.

MATISSE: *The Young Sailor.*
1906.

Oil on canvas, 39⅜ x 31⅞".
Collection Mr. and Mrs.
Jacques Gelman, Mexico City.
See color plate, page 22

AS EARLY as 1904 Henri Matisse began his search for new fields of expression, using thin, flat, colored surfaces, framed in a drawing of heavy lines—to oppose Pointillism, the last stronghold of Impressionism. The movement which was to be called Fauvism was sponsored by a number of young painters who felt the necessity of avoiding the impasse to which Impressionism and Pointillism had brought them. But Matisse, like all pioneers, was more than a theoretician of the moment. His first important reaction was in the treatment of form, starting from natural representation. He purposely ignored all conventions of anatomy and perspective in order to introduce whatever drawing he felt adequate to give maximum values to the flat hues of colors inserted within the intentional outlines. Coming just after the recognition of van Gogh, Cézanne, and Seurat, Matisse's idea was a deliberate attempt to open new roads in the physics of painting. Around 1908 he showed several large compositions which contained all the elements of his masterly conception. Perspective had been discarded and replaced by the relationship of strong forms which produced a three-dimensional effect of its own. Figures and trees were indicated with heavy lines, building the arabesque adjusted to the flat areas of color. The ensemble created a new scenery in which the objective composition appeared only as a remote guide. Ever since these early achievements, Matisse had added to his physical treatment of painting a very subtle chemistry of brushwork which amplified the completeness of his latest work.

Marcel Duchamp

MATISSE: *View of Collioure.*
1908.

Oil on canvas, 35⅞ x 24⅞".
Collection Mr. and Mrs.
Jacques Gelman, Mexico City

MOST OF Matisse's portraits, at least of the period of 1908–10, are scarcely portraits at all in the strictest sense of the word. Like those of Cézanne they are not so much characterizations on a psychological level as realizations of form. The same may be said generally of the picture of a pretty model, the *Girl with Green Eyes* painted in 1909. Here the figure is demurely frontal in pose, shifted only a little to the left to avoid a static, axial symmetry. But though the pose is quieter than that of the *Greta Moll*, not to mention the *Red Madras*, the activity of color and pattern in the *Girl with Green Eyes* is carried through both costume and background. The bright orange embroidered Chinese robe is seen against red to the left, green to the right. Instead of a figured textile behind the head, Matisse has placed a shelf of objects—his cast of a Parthenon torso and three strongly ornamented vases—against a light green background. The head of the model rises between these active shapes, her auburn hair guarding her pale face with its bright green eyes. The *Girl with Green Eyes* is remarkable among Matisse's portraits for its charm of subject, color verging on prettiness, and especially for its richness of pigment.

Alfred H. Barr, Jr.

MATISSE: *Girl with Green Eyes.*
1909.
Oil on canvas, 26 x 20".
San Francisco Museum of Art.
Harriet Lane Levy Bequest

IN THE GRAY cold of a Parisian winter, Matisse painted this austere, simplified figure which is diametrically opposed to the colorful, sensuous freedom of his earlier pictures. Warmth and hedonism have been replaced by a rigorous linear style and sober gray, near-monochrome palette. Strong line defines the massive columnar weight of the figure, tapering from heavy stool to solid, slightly rounded body to oval head on a straight neck. An equally heavy but less expressive line is used to describe the other two objects. The composition is reduced to a minimum; not an extraneous detail mars the ascetic restraint. The vase painting on the wall, by Matisse's then teen-aged son, Pierre, repeats the figure, in a symmetrical placement as well as in form. (*Woman on a High Stool* served a similar function two years later in the great *Piano Lesson* in The Museum of Modern Art.) A brief transition between the strict verticality of these two elements and the table's horizontal is effected by the sheet of paper which acts as a diagonal *repoussoir* and in turn duplicates the angle at which the stool is set.

Lucy R. Lippard

MATISSE: *Woman on a High Stool.* 1913-14.

Oil on canvas, 57⅞ x 37⅝".
The Museum of Modern Art, New York.
Gift of Mr. and Mrs. Samuel A. Marx,
the latter retaining life interest

WHAT MATISSE wrote and what Matisse said are important not only to students of art but to anyone concerned with visual perception. His observations were vivid and consistent, and they ring with clarity. Even in casual conversations, such as that quoted below, he was eloquent.

Some sixty years ago, Matisse was interviewed by an American lady. His remarks informally addressed to "the American people" are not inappropriate here. It was in the spring of 1913, the time of the Armory Show in New York, and Miss Clara T. MacChesney visited Matisse at Issy-les-Moulineaux. She expected "a long-haired, slovenly dressed, eccentric man." She was disappointed and said so. Quite frankly she did not admire "a huge, gaudy-hued canvas" and asked, "Don't you recognize harmony of color?"

Matisse, almost with indignation, replied: "I certainly do think of harmony of color, and of composition, too. Drawing is for me the art of being able to express myself with line. When an artist or student draws a nude figure with painstaking care, the result is drawing, and not emotion.

"I never use pastels or watercolors, and I only make studies from models, not to use in a picture—*mais pour me nourrir*—to strengthen my knowledge; and I never work from a previous sketch or study. I now draw with feeling, and not anatomically." Matisse added, parenthetically, "I know how to draw 'correctly,' having studied form for so long." He concluded: " Oh, do tell the American people that I am a normal man; that I am a devoted husband and father, that I have three fine children, that I go to the theater, ride horseback, have a comfortable home, a fine garden, that I love flowers, just like any other man."

After 1920, landscapes are infrequent in Matisse's art. Among the last paintings of his beloved south of France is this view of the road to Montalban, near Nice. The picture, along with others of the out-of-doors, was shown in Paris soon after it was completed in 1918. Early in May, Matisse asked his old and good friend, the painter Charles Camoin, "How did you find my small landscapes at Bernheim's Gallery? Did Félix Fénéon seem pleased? These are just small things that relax the mind, simple *détentes*. As perhaps you may have noticed, I tried to play with earth tones. I use cadmium and vermilion only accidentally. . . ."

W.S.L.

MATISSE: *Montalban*. 1918.
Oil on canvas, 29½ x 36½".
Private collection, France

FLESH, with various exotic trappings, would be a continual subject in the 1920s and 1930s. Painting from nature, Matisse was trying to relive an impossibly voluptuous dream. Yet the issue was crucial for an art such as his, and he had never faced it directly. As always, he was quite clear about his preoccupation: "My models . . . are the principal theme in my work. I depend entirely on my model whom I observe at liberty, and then I decide on the pose that best suits her nature. When I take a new model I guess the appropriate pose from the abandoned attitudes of repose, and then I become the slave of that pose. I often keep these girls for years, until the interest is exhausted."

He was evolving the form of dream that could be depended on to last. The flesh proved transitory, indeed incongruous, but the fantasy of delight spread to embrace everything. "The emotional interest aroused in me by them does not necessarily appear in the representation of their bodies. Often it is rather in the lines, through qualities distributed over the whole canvas or paper, forming the orchestration or architecture. But not everyone sees this. Perhaps it is sublimated voluptuousness, and that may not yet be visible to everyone."

As usual, he knew himself well. His burst of unblushing self-indulgence contributed something indispensable. The wholeness of his pictures came more and more to possess a distributed, sublimated voluptuousness. The final achievement had a pervasive quality of sensual fulfillment that was new to his work.

Lawrence Gowing

MATISSE: *The Artist and His Model.* 1919.
Oil on canvas, 23⅝ x 28¾".
Collection Dr. Ruth M. Bakwin, New York

ETRETAT is a Norman fishing village set on a brief stretch of beach between cliffs which look across the Channel to England. When Matisse spent a few weeks there following his return from London in midsummer 1920, he found a whole new range of stimulating subjects to see and paint.

The soft chalky cliff to the west of Etretat beach has been hollowed out by the sea to form a natural arch vaguely resembling an elephant's trunk. The Elephant has been a subject for many earlier artists, notably Courbet and Monet, but none of them ever painted it with the variety of invention displayed by Matisse, who was perhaps inspired by Hokusai's *Thirty-Six Views of Fuji*.

The three largest of Matisse's Etretat paintings, the *Conger Eel*, the *Great Cliff at Etretat*, and the *Two Rays*, are the same size and very similar in composition. In the foreground a catch of fish lies on some seaweed; to the left rises a cliff, and beyond in the distance a second low-lying promontory terminates in the Elephant with its accompanying Needle. The *Two Rays* is perhaps the most developed of these in composition, with its beautiful balance of vertical cliff past which sweeps the great receding curve of beach. The dark still life in the foreground is curiously answered by the remote black wedge of sail; otherwise the colors are pale tans, greens, and aquamarines.

Alfred H. Barr, Jr.

MATISSE: *Two Rays*. 1920.
Oil on canvas, 36¼ x 28¾".
Norton Gallery of Art,
West Palm Beach

THE *Checker Game and Piano Music* of 1923 is even more complex than the *Moorish Screen* of late 1921, now at the Philadelphia Museum of Art. Again there are three patterns on the floor and two aggressively striking ones on the walls. In addition there are the stripes of the tablecloth and the boys' blazers, the bright spots of hardware on the chest of drawers, the pictures on the wall, the violins hanging on the clothespress, the rosettes on either side of the sheet music, and, for good measure, the squares of the checkerboard are gratuitously repeated on the base of Michelangelo's *Slave!* Such an inventory may help one to understand Matisse's self-set problem in composing such a picture. Furthermore he had deepened the perspective and introduced a definite sense of light and cast shadow which were largely absent in the *Moorish Screen*. These suggestions of depth and light, though they add visual complexity, actually help to stabilize the composition: the far corner of the room is not only emphasized by the strong perspective diagonal of the rug border at the left but is also weighted by the ballasting clothespress. Around this armoire the other three masses—the piano group, the table group, and the chest of drawers—are disposed. They form the other three corners of a virtual "square-on-plan." A comparison with a remarkably similar subject, *The Painter's Family* of a dozen years before (in the Museum of Western Art, Moscow), is enlightening, particularly in the handling of space. Doubtless the later and smaller painting displays greater virtuosity in combining Eastern decorative patternizing with Western traditions of pictorial depth and directional lighting.

Matisse was of course conscious of the resemblance in subject between *The Painter's Family* of 1911 and the *Checker Game and Piano Music* of 1923—although in the later picture a model and her two brothers have taken the place of Mme Matisse, Marguerite, Jean, and Pierre. Indeed he may have intended an informal demonstration of the changes which the years had brought in his technical and aesthetic goals.

Alfred H. Barr, Jr.

MATISSE: *Checker Game and Piano Music.* 1923.

Oil on canvas, 29 x 36½".
Collection Mr. and Mrs.
Alexandre P. Rosenberg, New York

FROM NICE in April 1942, Matisse wrote his son Pierre that he had had a veritable *floraison* in his drawing and hoped soon to achieve the same thing in his painting. He worked in bed in his apartment in the Hotel Regina in Nice. One of his best-known canvases of the period is the *Dancer and Armchair*. Both the model in her blue costume and the curious chair Matisse painted again and again. These paintings of 1942 are conversation pieces but with an empty chair, or rather a chair holding various still-life assemblies. The chair, however, is of a *rocaille* design in carved wood so lively and so "organic" that it easily holds its own against the figure.

The variety of color, as one can see from Matisse's own color analysis, is extremely limited. Not counting the small, rather pale spots of orange and green fruits, there are only six hues: the lemon yellow of both chairs; the black of the floor; the whites of the coffee cup, the dancer's costume, and the stripes of floor and background; the strong blue of the wall, the costume, and the arms of the chair; the whitened cadmium red flesh tones of the dancer, and the bright cadmium red of her chair frame. Other paintings of the same period are very much more complex in color.

Alfred H. Barr, Jr.

MATISSE: *Dancer and Armchair.* **1942.**

Oil on canvas, 19⅞ x 25⅞".
Private collection, France

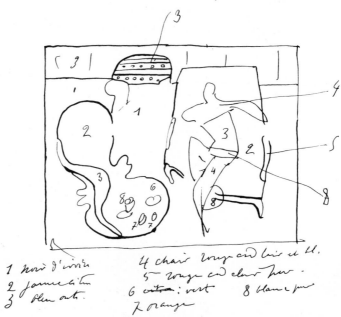

1 noir d'ivoire
2 jaune citron
3 bleu outr.
4 chair rouge and bleu et bl.
5 rouge and clair pur.
6 citron : vert
7 orange
8 blanc pur

MATISSE discerned a method, which has now become the method of virtually all painting. Deliberately basing painting on reactions to painting, he was setting in motion the modern feedback—the closed circuit within which the painter's intuition operates, continually intensifying qualities that are inherent. Whoever feels the radiance of Matisse's last works is experiencing the intensity that came from isolating what was intrinsic not only to a personality but to a whole tradition, and the communally conditioned reflex on which it depends.

When he painted his last great series of interiors, he was ready not only to sum up all his works but to add to it something of dazzling originality. The color floods the *Large Interior in Red* as it did his *Red Studio* (in The Museum of Modern Art, New York) nearly forty years earlier. But the meaning is different. The things in the room, not only the pictures on the wall but the flowers that bloom in a slight iridescent haze on the table, retain their own real quality. They remain whole, as if preserved in redness, with a new and permanent existence. Even the diagonal march of space across the floor and up into the pictures is linked with a pattern of coinciding edges, connecting tables to chairs and flowers to picture, so that both are seen as natural properties of the picture's flatness and redness. We become aware that we are in the presence of the reconciliation that is only within the reach of great painters in old age. The canvas radiates it. The redness overflows and people standing in front of the picture are seen to have it reflected on them. They are included in it; they share in a natural condition of things and of painting.

Lawrence Gowing

MATISSE: *Large Interior in Red.* 1948.
Oil on canvas, 57½ x 38¼".
Musée National d' Art Moderne, Paris.
See color plate, page 23

EXPRESSIONISM in FRANCE and GERMANY

IN THE SUMMER of 1905, Derain joined Matisse in Collioure on the southwest coast of France; and he was among the group whose paintings, shown at the Salon d'Automne in the fall of that year, profoundly shocked the critics by their "formless confusion of colors, blue, red, yellow, green, splotches of pigment crudely juxtaposed; the barbaric and naïve sport of a child who plays with a box of colors he has just got as a Christmas present." Matisse and his circle of artists were shortly dubbed Fauves ("wild beasts"). Some years later, Derain wrote: "Fauvism was our ordeal by fire . . . Colors became charges of dynamite. They were expected to discharge light . . . The great merit of this method was to free the picture from all imitative and conventional contact." Unlike many of the Fauves, however, Derain was determined to paint in terms of volumetric form as well as in decorative patterns of color.

The vehement brushstrokes recall those of van Gogh, one of the major early influences on Derain's art; but the bright, unnaturalistic color probably owes more to the sitter himself, who befriended and encouraged the younger artist and was responsible for persuading his parents to allow him to become a full-time painter.

Helen M. Franc

DERAIN: *Henri Matisse.* 1905.
Oil on canvas, 18⅛ x 13¾".
The Trustees of the Tate Gallery,
London.
See color plate, page 21

THIS IS one of three portraits of Matisse which Derain painted, in and out of doors, in 1905. Its psychological intensity is uncharacteristic of Fauve painting. The Tate Gallery also owns Matisse's portrait of Derain painted at the same place, at the same time.

W.S.L.

COLLIOURE, a charming old fortified seaport nestling between the sparkling Mediterranean and the foothills of the Pyrenees, is one of the sacred places of modern art. For it was the virtual birthplace of Fauve painting—that revolutionary exaltation of pure color; the first great aesthetic movement of the twentieth century—and the inspiration of Matisse and Derain in 1905–06, a place as central to their art at that moment as the valley of the Seine had been to the Impressionists, or Provence to Cézanne and van Gogh.

Here we have Derain's view of the little town itself, a scene that obviously delighted him, what with the lively figures of sailors and fishermen at work and play in the foreground, the sailboats marshaled up against the quay, and, across the tiny harbor, the backdrop of toy houses. Note, too, the tricolor waving proudly in the center of the barricade of red masts. Rightly so. This brilliant painting is a French victory. It could be a stage set (Derain liked to dramatize subject matter) and impresses one by the intensity with which it is depicted, bathed in what Derain called "a golden light that does away with shadows." Or, as he explained further, "Every shadow is a whole world of clarity and luminosity which contrasts with sunlight; what is known as reflection."

In works such as this, Derain was rebelling against the Impressionists' careful analyses of nature and radically disregarding the rules of conventional draftsmanship, making color itself, squeezed straight from the tube, evoke light, space, and things seen. Breaking with the past, and the present, however, was no gesture of defiance for its own sake. The Fauves thought out their innovative style carefully and not, at moments, without anxiety. Later on Derain explained how the revolution came about. "Fauvism," he wrote, "was our ordeal by fire . . . Those were the years of photography. This may have influenced us, and played a part in our reaction against anything resembling a snapshot of life. No matter how far we moved away from things, in order to observe them and transpose them at our leisure, it was never far enough. Colors became charges of dynamite. They were expected to discharge light. It was a fine idea, in its freshness, that everything could be raised above the real. It was serious too . . . The great merit of this method was to free the picture from all imitative and conventional contact."

Stuart Preston

LIKE MOST new aesthetic departures encountered for the first time, Fauvism appeared to have sprung into being sui generis, or, at least, without immediately obvious stylistic antecedents. Again like most, however, it drew on many sources for its existence—sources now recognizable in the perspective of time and from fuller knowledge of the state of avant-garde painting at the turn of the century.

Derain is judged to be, and correctly, a highly eclectic artist, more susceptible than others to reflecting in his work manifold, often contradictory influences. *The Red Sails*, painted about the same time as the *View of Collioure* (page 111), is not as exclusively a Fauve picture, differing in character and in technique. Whereas *View of Collioure* makes a brisk, jocular, idiosyncratic statement of plain facts, *The Red Sails* is ambiguous, solemn, emotional, dependent intellectually on Symbolism, and owing much, technically, to van Gogh and to Signac, each of whom contributed importantly to Fauvism.

From Symbolism is derived the poetic idea, embodied here, of the material world vanishing into the unknown, in this case by the boats setting out to sea as the sun goes down. This is a literary and mystical concept clothed in sensuous visual form, of which numerous correspondences can be found both in Symbolist poetry—Mallarmé —and in late Romantic French music—in Debussy's haunting, melancholy song *Beau Soir*.

Technically, Derain does not employ here the staccato, telegraphic painterly style of *View of Collioure*. Color, which is as bright but more fervid and of greater emotional depth, is applied in small juxtaposed dabs of paint which fuse into a single radiance in the eye of the beholder. By this means—the Pointillist style, as developed by Seurat and by Signac—extraordinary luminosity is achieved. It must be noticed that pure color, as used here, is not abstract color. As Matisse, the dominant Fauve, repeatedly declared, color "must serve expression." *The Red Sails* is an Expressionist painting, Pointillist in technique, and owing to van Gogh its forcefulness as well as the lovely spiraling rhythm of the mainsail of the big boat in the foreground, a pattern of curves turned into a continuous movement. Altogether, *The Red Sails* is an untypical Derain. But then, one wonders, what painting by Derain is "typical"?

Stuart Preston

DERAIN: *The Red Sails.*
1905–06.
Oil on canvas, 32 x 39½".
Private collection, Houston

IT IS SIGNIFICANT that many of the pictures which inaugurated Rouault's personal style should have reflected the frenzied preoccupation with sin and redemption expressed in Léon Bloy's *Le Désespéré* and *La Femme Pauvre*. It seems likely, too, that Rouault's choice of prostitutes as symbols of earthly degradation—and also as subjects for instant redemption through suffering—was inspired by Bloy. Prostitutes had played a key part in Bloy's writing and life. He had loved and converted to his own passionate Catholicism two women of the streets, later used as heroines of his novels. (A parallel with the life of Vincent van Gogh is suggested.) In Bloy's novels, prostitutes are the absolute counterparts of saints, and he made abundantly clear that he was interested only in extremes of conduct and character.

Rouault's studies of prostitutes, executed about this time, are often in watercolor, which he used as a major medium throughout his early career. It may have been watercolor which freed him from the elaborate chiaroscuro and brown tonality of his years in Gustave Moreau's studio and enriched the blue palette of his landscapes painted between 1898 and 1902. He worked now with summary directness, blocking in the forms with strong, antinaturalistic highlights. The figures were sometimes spattered rather than modeled into existence, and he frequently used a broken-line technique. The interiors which house his subjects are defined by a linear perspective which in later paintings was to be abandoned for an atmospheric manipulation of space through juxtaposed tones.

A relation between these watercolors and Toulouse-Lautrec's art has been mentioned by several critics. But few of Rouault's early paintings show the sensual relish of decadence for its own satanic sake which characterized Toulouse-Lautrec's work. To the latter's cynicism, Rouault opposed tears and rage. He was not interested in the detailed decline of the flesh which so inevitably fascinated the crippled Toulouse-Lautrec. He sought the grimace and posture of irrevocable martyrdom. And he himself has indignantly denied the influence of the Degas–Toulouse-Lautrec tradition, explaining his change in direction as the result of a profound upheaval within himself: "I underwent then a moral crisis of the most violent sort. I experienced things which cannot be expressed by words. And I began to paint with an outrageous lyricism which disconcerted everybody . . . It was not the influence of Lautrec, Degas, or the moderns which inspired me, but an inner necessity and the perhaps unconscious desire to fall full-length into conventional religious subject matter."

James Thrall Soby

ROUAULT: *Girl at a Mirror.* 1906.

Watercolor on cardboard, 27⅝ x 20⅞".
Musée National d'Art Moderne, Paris

ROUAULT: *Two Prostitutes.* 1906.

Watercolor and pastel on cardboard, 26½ x 24¼".
Collection E. M. Bakwin

OF ALL the Fauves, the "wild beasts" (pages 86, 108, 234), Vlaminck was unquestionably the wildest. Proud of his lack of discipline, of his muscular strength, of his uncouthness, he reveled in an attitude of revolt and of contempt for everything that involved learning or reason. He avoided nearby Paris and the company of other painters, instead painting ardently with his comrade Derain in Chatou, which became to Fauvism what Argenteuil had been to Impressionism.

In 1901, Vlaminck had received a profound shock from the first large Vincent van Gogh exhibition ever held in Paris; this was for him an almost dolorous revelation. In spite of all his admiration for van Gogh's canvases, he immediately recognized in him a formidable adversary. Here was a man who had had the same aspirations as himself, who had translated in his work the same torments and exaltations, the same visions and impressions with which he was struggling. And he had translated them with pure colors and brushstrokes so expressive that all his emotions seemed to lie bare on his canvases. Compared with the pursuit of delicate light effects characteristic of the Impressionists, whose pictures Vlaminck had seen occasionally in Paris, van Gogh suddenly burst forth with an unprecedented intensity of color and design.

Back in Chatou, Vlaminck began to assimilate van Gogh's lesson. "I heightened all the tones," he wrote later, "I transposed into an orchestration of pure colors all the feelings of which I was conscious. I was a barbarian, tender and full of violence. I translated by instinct, without any method, not merely an artistic truth but above all a human one. I crushed and botched the ultramarines and vermilions, though they were very expensive and I had to buy them on credit."

To Vlaminck, Fauvism "was not an invention, an attitude, but a manner of being, of acting, of thinking, of breathing." More robust, more ready to follow instinct unimpeded by doubts or intellectual preoccupations, he attained a violence of assertion which went beyond that of all his friends. "To create presupposes pride," he later explained, "an immeasurable pride perhaps! You have to have confidence in yourself, to feel the exclusive need of expressing what you feel independently of any exterior support. It is possible also that this frank ignorance, this unconscious simplicity, preserves us from experiments in which we might lose ourselves."

In spite of the powerful creative urge which presided over Vlaminck's feverish output of those years—or possibly because of it—he did not always attain a complete balance of purpose and expression; but where this is achieved, as in the present canvas, the vigorous qualities of his paintings are like the triumphant sound of trumpets.

John Rewald

VLAMINCK: *Tugboat at Chatou.* 1906.
Oil on canvas, 19¾ x 25¾".
Collection Mr. and Mrs.
John Hay Whitney, New York

IN GERMANY before World War I, several groups of artists allied themselves against the Establishment. In retrospect, two are most clearly remembered: Die Brücke (The Bridge), page 122, and Der Blaue Reiter (The Blue Rider), which proclaimed itself in Munich in 1911. It is almost impossible to overestimate the importance of the latter's single publication, *The Blue Rider Almanac*, issued in 1912. The editors of the almanac, Franz Marc and Kandinsky, organized exhibitions with other painters, among them August Macke, Jawlensky, and Klee. Feininger was also invited to exhibit. The war dissolved the group; Macke and Marc were killed in action.

The Blaue Reiter was a less structured and more cosmopolitan association than the Brücke. Kandinsky and Jawlensky were Russian, Klee had been born in Switzerland, Feininger in the United States. Also, the Blaue Reiter acknowledged the School of Paris and was in dialogue with the Russian avant-garde. In 1907 in Paris, Jawlensky worked with Matisse, and he met the French painter once again, briefly, in 1911. Jawlensky had left Russia in 1896 to study painting in Munich. There he had met his fellow countryman Kandinsky, with whom he worked in close association in 1908 and 1909. They remained in Bavaria, and in close contact, until 1914.

Jawlensky's first mature style, of which *The Gardener* is a superb if least typical example, was developed in 1908 and lasted through 1913. This portrait has a psychological intensity rare in his work but characteristic of Expressionism, particularly in Germany. The old man stares straight at the spectator who, in turn, sees him close up as in a photograph. A feeling of sadness is emphasized by the details of his visage: the deep furrows of the forehead, the downward thrust of the nose, and the depressed corners of the mouth.

Color is unnatural but not arbitrary. The relationship between primaries becomes most active in the areas of the eyes where blue and yellow and red, each outlined in black, appear side by side. The yellow background, the blue hair, and the red face repeat similarly the same juxtapositions. In another painting of the same man, identical in size, Jawlensky reversed the colors of the background and beard, and the hair of the head is painted in their complementary color, green. Jawlensky's brushwork is evident, even crude. Here, it contributes to the rugged aspect of the sitter.

W.S.L.

JAWLENSKY: *The Gardener.*
1912.
Oil on cardboard, 20⅞ x 19⅜".
Milwaukee Art Center Collection.
Gift of
Mr. and Mrs. Harry Lynde Bradley

1913 WAS a year of flowering in Kandinsky's art. By then master of the abstract style which he had been evolving since 1909, he was in perfect control of the full range of his pictorial means.

Kandinsky's first *Improvisations* in 1909 had reversed the process of his early landscapes; now an inner pictorial vision was superimposed upon the exterior world. Representational references were abbreviated to mere hieroglyphs of objective form—"reminiscences," as Will Grohmann called them—which can be determined largely through association with earlier works. The theme for Kandinsky had lost its supremacy; pure color had replaced it.

Kandinsky had inherited the Symbolists' interest in the synaesthetic aspect of color, its ability to conjure parallel sensations and associations on senses other than visual—blue, for instance, his favorite color, could suggest the sound of a flute. Ultimately, it was the autonomous psychological power of color that fascinated Kandinsky.

The beautiful *Little Pleasures* of 1913 celebrates the emancipation of color. The similarities to the objective world are distorted, their natural relations canceled, their normal space suppressed. Free, sensuous play of color reigns supreme.

Iconographically, however, it is possible to recognize certain of his favorite "reminiscences": at center, steeply rising mountains atop which sit the "golden-headed" forms of "Mother Moscow"; weaving in and out of the left side, three riders in blue; at lower left, a couple walking toward a magically waving copse; at lower right, three persons rowing on a furiously heaving sea. These clues, to Hans Röthel, identify the "little pleasures" of the title—riding, rowing, loving.

Kandinsky seems to have formulated the composition of the picture as early as 1911. The following year he dealt with the same theme in a painting on glass. He also produced two remarkably free watercolors, which are preparatory studies for the final painting in oil, and one astounding drawing. The drawing, in black and white and dated 1913, is composed of rigidly geometric forms in dynamic interrelation; it is an extraordinary premonition of the later work of the Bauhaus years and, specifically, of the painting *Backward Glance* (1924), which still belongs to the artist's widow.

None of the iconographic or formal references, however, can explain or exhaust the magic of the 1913 oil. The fairy-tale "balladesque" mood, the joyful rhythm of form and color—all flow into a mysterious, hovering whole, inviting the mystical "entering into" the painting that Kandinsky so desired.

Susana Leval

KANDINSKY: *Little Pleasures.*
1913.
Oil on canvas, 43½ x 47½".
The Solomon R. Guggenheim Museum,
New York.
See color plate, page 28

IN 1905 in Dresden, three young students, Kirchner, Erich Heckel, and Karl Schmidt-Rottluff, banded together to form the first group of German Expressionists, Die Brücke (The Bridge). They were joined by a few other artists, including Nolde (page 124), but until World War I dissolved the group, the founding trio remained its core. They exhibited together, published portfolios, issued proclamations and even membership cards.

The formation of the Brücke coincided with the much looser association of the Fauves in France. Both groups were deeply influenced by the Post-Impressionists and by primitive art. Both exploited unnatural color and bold distortion in their drawing. But the more intimate, even daily, association of the German artists gave the Brücke cohesion as a brotherhood. In Germany, they constituted an avant-garde reaction against Impressionism, which was already growing academic by 1905.

W.S.L.

KIRCHNER, the leader of the Brücke and an early enthusiast of primitive art, evolved his most potent style by 1912. In *The Street*, a harsh psychological expressionism is implemented by acrid colors and rapid movement, inspired by the febrile gaiety of prewar Berlin. Figures and space are distorted into a boldly patterned surface that centers on a driving vertical wedge-shape: a flame- or arrow-form like a Gothic tower —another of Kirchner's favorite subjects. Kirchner's theme—the desperate alienation of modern man—was borne out by his own life. The war left him a sick man, and he spent the rest of his life in Switzerland, where he painted landscapes in a gentler and far less forceful manner. In 1938, with another war approaching, he committed suicide.

Lucy R. Lippard

KIRCHNER: *Street, Berlin.*
1913.
Oil on canvas, 47½ x 35⅞".
The Museum of Modern Art, New York

DIE BRUCKE had a more emotional, more personal basis than the short-lived French group of Fauves, and painters like Nolde continued to work in this style throughout their lives. Nolde possessed a raw, childlike vision, with an emphasis upon spontaneity, sensuous but arbitrary color, and freedom of execution. In his memoirs he wrote that "the quicker a painting is done, the better it is . . . In art I fight for unconscious creation. Labor destroys painting." In 1913, when his interest in primitive art was at a peak, Nolde went to New Guinea as a pictorial reporter for the government, traveling across Russia and Siberia. When he returned, he made a series of paintings from his travel sketches, among them several heads of stoic Russians painted in an almost brutal manner with strong, somber colors and a composition that stresses weight. Here the two heads are squeezed into the rectangular format in a direct, even uncomfortable confrontation—as if thrust forward in support of an argument. The two triangular shapes with their straight band of brows and eyes recall African masks, though in a very different way from the use of similar sources by Picasso or Modigliani.

Lucy R. Lippard

NOLDE: *Russian Peasants.*
1915.
Oil on canvas, 29 x 35½".
The Museum of Modern Art, New York.
The Matthew T. Mellon
Foundation Fund

IN THE SUMMER of 1914, at the age of thirty, Max Beckmann enlisted in the medical corps of the German army. He was witness to the full horror of human carnage. The experience overwhelmed him and was to be a terrible inspiration. His own health and mind devastated, he himself was hospitalized.

After his discharge from the army, his character and his art completely changed. Rather than return to Berlin, he settled in Frankfurt, and he reversed his style, portraying form in an Expressionist and angular manner with an increasingly personal vision fevered alternately by passion and despair. *The Descent from the Cross* was his first important picture in his new style. Although the composition shows the influence of Northern Gothic art, it is perhaps also indebted to a Fra Angelico altarpiece of the same subject which Beckmann had studied in Florence in 1906.

The death of Christ on the Cross is the central image in Christian art, the visual focus of contemplation and prayer. The Deposition, the episode which succeeds the Crucifixion, is mentioned in all Gospels. The Crucifixion lends itself, traditionally, to a symmetrical treatment. The very act of the Deposition suggests an alternative solution, and here the attenuated body of Christ stretches diagonally across the picture. Spatial relations are compressed and no single pattern of perspective is followed. Like medieval artists, Beckmann portrays the Virgin swooning at the sight of the Deposition. The weeping figure, however, wears a blouse of red, a color usually associated with the other kneeling figure, Mary Magdalene. Behind them is St. John. The two men who lower His body appear as wracked as Christ—traditionally, they should be the richly clad Joseph of Arimathea and the youthful Nicodemus. Beckmann also alludes to the eclipse of the sun and moon, which according to Matthew, Mark, and Luke occurred at the moment of the Crucifixion itself.

In the same year, Beckmann painted *Christ and the Woman Taken in Adultery* (in the St. Louis Art Museum), a pendant to *The Descent from the Cross*. Both pictures are thinly painted and the colors are, for Beckmann, unusually subdued. A year later, he engraved the Deposition as a drypoint.

The Descent was purchased by the Frankfurt museum and was subsequently confiscated by the Nazis, who featured it in the exhibition "Degenerate Art" in Munich in 1937. Curt Valentin, a great friend of Beckmann's as well as his dealer, acquired the painting and subsequently bequeathed it to The Museum of Modern Art.

W.S.L.

BECKMANN: *The Descent from the Cross.* 1917.
Oil on canvas, 59½ x 50¾".
The Museum of Modern Art, New York.
Curt Valentin Bequest

THE GERMAN painter Lovis Corinth, more than twenty years the senior of his compatriots Beckmann and Kirchner, was born in the generation of Seurat and Ensor. For many years he painted successfully in an academic style with an extraordinary, if pedestrian, technical facility. He excelled at portraiture and received countless commissions. He also painted nudes and illustrated classical and biblical myths. His renditions were literal, often sensual, and sometimes extravagant.

When he reached the age of fifty-five, shortly before World War I, Corinth's art underwent a profound and rapid change for which there seems to be neither biographical nor spiritual reason. His brushwork became more free, even virtuosic, his attitude more introspective and at the same time sympathetic. The liberation and development of his later style was undoubtedly influenced by the example of younger artists, Expressionist painters such as Beckmann and Nolde.

Corinth painted some of the greatest portraits of the twentieth century, and, like so many Expressionists, he was obsessed by his own image, which he depicted over and over again in paintings, drawing, and prints. Beckmann's anguished search might well have been Corinth's own: "It is the quest of our ego that drives us along the eternal and never-ending journey we must all explore. What am I? This is the question that constantly persecutes and torments me."

This over-life-size representation of himself is one of the last of Corinth's many self-portraits. It was painted a few months before his death. It is rare in the art of the twentieth century that an artist can capture such a deep and convincing feeling for the human personality. The comparison which Corinth invites to Rembrandt is denied by the gray and tan colors of the painting.

W.S.L.

CORINTH: *Self-Portrait.* 1924.
Oil on canvas, 39⅜ x 31⅝".
The Museum of Modern Art, New York.
Gift of Curt Valentin

THE LAST OF Soutine's pictures in an important set or series were landscapes featuring trees. Tree worship is a cult anciently established in the Lithuanian part of Russia. In Soutine's youth there were still arboreal rites in villages not far removed from Smilovitchi (where he was born, near Minsk), and at the foot of any very noble specimen in the countryside one might find offerings . . . In any case no other notable contemporary painter has offered us portraiture of so many individual trees of distinct character, with strong romantic implications.

The *Alley of Trees* was painted at Grands Prés near Chartres; it was a theme which he undertook several times, always effectively. Painted in extraordinarily thick impasto, as years before in Céret, apparently they are poplar trees, growing in the collective shape of a very tall arch or portal, on which the uppermost twigs and the brightness of the sky seem to ramble in delicate liveliness. The light gleams through the boughs, a mysterious little crimson cottage shines out from beyond the tree trunks, and two miniature personages somewhat grandly gesture as they proceed on the narrow road.

Monroe Wheeler

SOUTINE: *Alley of Trees.* 1936.
Oil on canvas, 30⅛ x 27⅜".
Collection Lady Harlech, London

A VIOLENT stimulus produces a trauma in an organism. So too a work of art—if it really is a work of art—can create a genuine experience, a visual shock, in the consciousness of a receptive observer . . . I see creative art as a source, a spring, like Nature itself. I defend it as the constantly active, living material of thought. Had the politicians and generals not spared a few of the testimonies of art, what, today, would we make of history with its long record of millions slaughtered for the sake of abstract ideas?

Oskar Kokoschka

KOKOSCHKA:
Port of Hamburg. 1951.
Oil on canvas, 35¾ x 47½".
The Museum of Modern Art
New York.
Rose Gershwin Fund

IN 1924, the Czech painter Kokoschka left Dresden, where he had lived for several years, and began a decade of restless travel. He eventually settled in England and, in 1947, became a British subject. Some of his most memorable paintings are vistas of great ports—London, Amsterdam, Marseilles, Venice, and Istanbul.

Hamburg, on the North Sea, is Germany's greatest port. During World War II, sixty percent of its harbor installations were demolished and fifty-five thousand people killed. Today reconstruction is complete and new building continues.

In 1951, Kokoschka painted the portrait of his friend Max Brauer, a Social Democrat and then mayor of Hamburg. Later, during the summer, he composed this tempestuous, sweeping perspective of the port. The view, as so often in Kokoschka's landscapes, is from a high vantage, in this case the Bernhard Nocht Haus, a hospital for tropical diseases.

Kokoschka's dramatic vista shows in the foreground the quais at which all passenger boats dock. The land masses, at top left and bottom right, are the bank of the Elbe River. Across the water are the shipyards and, in the far distance at the right, the borough of Finkenwerder. The cupola domes the entrance to the old Elbe Tunnel, which like the railroad station of Hamburg was, curiously, not destroyed by the war. The spired church, which in reality could not appear here, is perhaps Kokoschka's own invention. The height of the view is emphasized by the seagull over the cupola. The bird hovers in the sky, below the spectator but above the panorama. Kokoschka had previously used such a device as early as 1927.

Color, for Kokoschka, has always meant intensification. Its function is not only dynamic, it also gives depth to space and widens the format of the picture frame which in all Kokoschka's landscapes is always horizontal.

W.S.L.

IN 1942 Jean Dubuffet decided to devote his full energies to painting. He was more than forty years of age and, like Gauguin and Matisse, his late decision to become an artist was a considered, irrevocable act.

For more than thirty years Dubuffet has experimented, relentlessly, with ideas and techniques in every medium he has chosen to explore. With astonishing inventiveness, he has varied the successful methods of his painting, printmaking, sculpture, and, most recently, architecture. In paint, as on paper, Dubuffet usually composes in series, and for each he develops special forms, perspectives, and colors. *Grand Jazz Band (New Orleans)* belongs to the first such series, begun early in 1943 and ending in the spring of 1945, which he later entitled *Marionettes of the City and Country*. It consists of more than four hundred paintings, drawings, and lithographs.

In Paris in December 1944, a few months after the Liberation, Dubuffet painted three *Jazz Bands*—*Dirty Style Blues, Black Chicago,* and, in this exhibition, *New Orleans,* the largest of the three. Early in the same year he had shown his work publicly for the first time. The exhibition aroused enormous controversy; the reaction, he noted, included "passionate admiration by some, vivid irritation on the part of most, scandal, violent disputes."

Of the *Jazz Bands* Dubuffet has written: "Grand concert. Choir of media. Chorus of all elements inspiring the artist's conception. Hence, reason and logic are singing. Passion, brutality, ferocity, all are singing. Weakness and cowardice too. In unison. And imagination, gratuitous invention, even absurd, incoherent. Obscure aspirations. Frenzy and madness. And at this very moment, the oil melts into colors, which muddy themselves as they come in contact with the surrounding colors, still damp. The hand tries to stop them. But all elements shout loudly, freely. At least in such a way that no restraint is visible; however there is a certain guidance, there is a conductor to direct this orchestra, flexible and subtle."

W.S.L.

DUBUFFET: *Grand Jazz Band (New Orleans)*. 1944.
Oil on canvas, 45⅛ x 57⅝".
Collection Mr. and Mrs.
Gordon Bunshaft, New York

CUBISM and ITS AFFINITIES

BETWEEN 1905 and 1910 Pablo Picasso, inspired by the primitive Negro sculpture introduced into Europe, was able to reject the heritage of the Impressionist and Fauve schools and to free himself from any immediate influence. This will be Picasso's main contribution to art: to have been able to start from a new source, and to keep this freshness with regard to whatever new expressions mark the different epochs of his career. Cubism, in itself, was an art movement of which Picasso was only a "pioneer." He never felt bound to follow through a theory of Cubism, even though he might have been responsible for its elaboration. Picasso, in each one of his facets, made clear his intention to keep free from preceding achievements. One of the important differences between Picasso and most of his contemporaries is that until the 1940s he never showed any sign of weakness or repetition in his uninterrupted flow of masterpieces. The only constant trend running through his work is an acute lyricism, which with time has changed into a cruel one. Every now and then the world looks for an individual on whom to rely blindly—such worship is comparable to a religious appeal and goes beyond reasoning. Thousands in quest of supernatural aesthetic emotion have turned to Picasso, who never let them down.

Marcel Duchamp

PICASSO never allowed himself to become completely absorbed by one influence and, in contrast to the powerful turbulent effect that Negro sculpture was having on his work at this time, we find in this composition a classical sense of order and geometric simplifications which Cézanne had shown in his analysis of forms in nature. The sobriety of the greens are reminiscent of Cézanne and also herald the coming discipline of Cubism.

Roland Penrose

PICASSO: *Landscape, La Rue des Bois.* 1908.
Oil on canvas, 39⅝ x 32⅛".
Collection Mr. and Mrs.
David Rockefeller, New York

IN THE MOST general terms, that whereas Picasso's Cubist paintings tend to be more pronouncedly linear, angular, immediate in the presentation, even sculptural in conception, Braque's are more painterly, lyrical, suave, and cohesive.

The effect of the alliance between the two men soon showed in Braque's work, notably in two superb still lifes, *Violin and Palette* and *Piano and Mandola*, painted during the winter of 1909–10. Here, coming closer to Picasso, Braque was much bolder in his formal analysis, so that his faceting is more elaborate, and he has broken the continuity of outlines in order to express volume through a series of interlocking cubes. Nevertheless the objects represented remain legible. The significance of this fragmentation was later accounted for by Braque when he said that it was a means of getting closer to objects "within the limits that painting would allow" and of establishing "space and movement in space." In other words, it was a way of reconciling his knowledge of a given three-dimensional surface of the canvas. But it is important to add that neither in the work of Braque nor of Picasso were any preliminary mathematical calculations involved in the cubifying process. . . .

Braque's two still lifes and Picasso's *Seated Woman* (page 143) represent the point at which the development of the technique of faceting—by which they were able to create volumes and make space tangible—caused the two artists to realize that they had to decide how they intended in the future to use color and light. In these three paintings both artists had used a limited but modulated palette of green, ocher, and gray and had lit parts of objects from different angles. In other words, they had paid no heed to local color and had imposed their pictorial will both on form and on light. Braque even underscored the resulting inconsistencies and sylistic innovations of Cubism by his ironic treatment of the nail on which the palette hangs at the top of the canvas. For he painted it in *trompe l'oeil*, completed by a regular shadow, thereby pointing a contrast between his own invented method and the familiar eye-fooling method of representing reality.

Douglas Cooper

BRAQUE: *Piano and Mandola.*
1909–10.

Oil on canvas, 36⅛ x 16⅞".
The Solomon R. Guggenheim Museum,
New York

BRAQUE: *Violin and Palette.*
1909–10.

Oil on canvas, 36¼ x 16⅞".
The Solomon R. Guggenheim Museum,
New York

IN 1910, Picasso's paintings became increasingly "hermetic." Their colors are consistently limited to brown and grays, and the forms are organized in shallow depth over the entire surface of the picture so as to avoid sudden rifts.

The construction of the figure is composed of facets among which it is still possible to detect clues as to the subject matter; but its essential merit lies in the freedom with which forms have been reorganized in an abstract manner.

The eye travels over a continuous play of semitransparent recessions and intrusions, occasionally picking up landmarks such as a head, a breast, the line of a shoulder or arm, and in its passage it can continually enjoy moving over surfaces that are convincingly definite and that create a reality of their own. The architecture of the human form reappears as a transparent scaffolding in which the interior and exterior are both apparent.

In most Cubist paintings of this period the denial of color results in a luminosity which radiates from the painting itself. Light appears to emanate from the forms rather than be projected from an exterior source.

The breaking up of the forms of objects so as to rebuild their structure with new significance became a basic principle of Cubism between 1910 and 1912.

Roland Penrose

PICASSO: *Portrait of a Woman.*
1910.

Oil on canvas, 39¾ x 32¼".
Collection Mrs. Gilbert W. Chapman,
New York

IN 1911 and 1912, the epochal years of Analytic Cubism, Picasso painted some twenty pictures in oval shapes. Their formats are equally vertical or horizontal, their subjects mostly still lifes. Braque favored the shape so much that he even painted pictures which were completely round. Indeed, both artists found an ovoid frame particularly appropriate. It enclosed as well as complemented the straight lines and angles of their compositions, which were generally structured on a central mass of rectangular planes. An ovoid format enhanced this vortex and, without empty edges, suppressed the four corners of a traditional frame.

What is seen? A still life arranged on a table. The subject, however, is relatively unimportant. Picasso's chief concern is the building of a pyramidal construction which concentrates on an architectural expression of form and which does not attempt to depict the factual reality of the objects. The still life is also arranged vertically, as if one might be looking at a picture which has been already painted and which has been propped up for viewing. At the very bottom of the oval appears the crank of an easel. Bottle and glass are transformed into a rhythmic cascade of straight lines. The objects have all but disappeared. One sees a knife, but where is the fork?

In this painting, as in the poems by Mallarmé, Valéry, and Picasso's close friend Apollinaire (all three also virtuosi of fragmentation), an extreme purism proceeds by destruction. The crystallization of the objects is contrasted and starkly relieved by the placement of easily legible letters and numbers. The black, painted block lettering and imitation stenciled numerals are formal, not contextural, elements of the composition. Torn from any literal meaning, they assume a fresh sense of being. They are, also, a prelude to collage. In pictures such as this and the earlier "portrait" (page 143), Picasso is at his most abstract, and Cubist analysis at its most extreme.

W.S.L.

PICASSO: *Bottle, Glass, and Fork.* 1912.

Oil on canvas, 28¾ x 21¼".
The Cleveland Museum of Art.
Purchase, Leonard C. Hanna, Jr.
Bequest

THE CZECH artist Kupka was the first painter in Paris systematically to explore the possibilities of abstraction. This portrait of his wife was begun about 1909 (when he was experimenting with Fauvist color), but was left unfinished until 1911, when he painted the vibrant planes which almost overwhelm the face.

At the same time Kupka was also painting other works with vertical planes which eliminated any figurative reference. He continued to explore this system until 1913, when he composed *Vertical Planes III* (now in the Prague National Gallery), the first large-scale geometric abstraction ever exhibited. This portrait, therefore, represents a moment when Kupka could look back over the figurative painting which had occupied him since the 1890s and which he would soon abandon.

Kupka, however, intended a deeper significance in the juxtaposition of the abstract and the figurative. He believed in the unity of the human spirit with the spiritual forces animating the cosmos. He found confirmation of this belief both in the fact that white light is composed of prismatic color and in the contemporary scientific discovery that matter is composed of energy, which may have determined him to replace the body with a tissue of vibrating prismatic colors. Kupka was also probably influenced by the spiritualist belief that every individual possesses an "aura" which indicates personality and which is perceptible to those endowed with spiritual "sight." He may have believed that his awareness of his wife's spiritual being dictated his shimmering immaterial colors. In this sense, the painting is a colored radiance, a literal illustration of a spiritualist belief. More importantly, it helped Kupka escape from illustration, for as he improvised the strokes of color, he became absorbed in the way that they formed coherent structures. He came to realize that such abstract structures contain their own meaning.

Kupka arrived at abstract art through the processes of painting rather than through theory, and thus achieved a profound understanding of the experience that is embodied in such art. He maintained that a work of art cannot communicate a specific idea, since the artist's idea is transformed by the creative process and by the spectator's response, but that it could awaken the spectator's consciousness of his own being by absorbing him in its unique physical reality. Although Kupka did not succeed in awakening such consciousness in this painting—the head draws attention to the existence of a specific person in such a way that one cannot appreciate the abstract forms—his awareness of why he was unsuccessful caused him to move to more firmly structured abstract paintings.

Virginia Spate

KUPKA: *Mme Kupka among Verticals.* 1911.
Oil on canvas, 53⅜ x 33⅝".
The Museum of Modern Art, New York.
Hillman Periodicals Fund

THE THEORETICIAN and, until his early death in 1916, the most important artist of the Futurist movement, Boccioni was concerned with a fusion of light, color, movement—even sounds and smells—associated with particular scenes. *The Laugh* is an early work, in which he had only begun to suggest such a synthesis. A first version, executed in 1910–11, was slashed by razor blades by irate visitors to the Exhibition of Free Art in Milan. This revision was made later in 1911, after Boccioni had seen the works of Picasso and Braque in Paris; it is probable that the areas of Cubist treatment (bottles, glasses seen from double angles, the rectilinear divisions) were added at that point. When *The Laugh* was shown in Berlin in 1912, a critic wrote that "the painter dances like a drunk around a woman's hat." The hat revolves again and again; the red flame of a cigarette being lit also recurs throughout the picture. The lady sits in a café with other figures, but they are largely dissolved in the path of her laugh—the real subject—which seems to roll out at the viewer in rounded, steplike forms.

Lucy R. Lippard

BOCCIONI: *The Laugh*. 1911.
Oil on canvas, 43⅜ x 57¼".
The Museum of Modern Art, New York.
Gift of Herbert and Nannette
Rothschild

"WE CHOOSE to concentrate our attention on things in motion because our modern sensibility is particularly qualified to grasp the idea of speed. Heavy, powerful motor cars rushing through the streets of our cities, dancers reflected in the fair ambience of light and color, airplanes flying above the heads of the excited throng . . . These sources of emotion satisfy our sense of a lyric and dramatic universe, better than do two pears and an apple."

Futurist Manifesto, 1912

WHEN THE younger Futurist painters in Milan were rushing to complete works for their Paris exhibition, Balla in Rome was quietly evolving his own ideas about the movement. His scurrying little dog on a leash is probably the first Futurist painting to display a genial sense of humor. "Dynamism" seems too formidable a word to describe such a delightful pattern of rhythmic motions. It is dynamism subjected to the same sensitivity to pattern, precision of touch, and subtlety of color to be found in Balla's earlier paintings. Not passion but acute observation determined its forms, and the painter made no effort to suggest that the dog was more than a dog or the leash more than a leash. The observer is not thrust into an intense situation, but allowed to enjoy in detachment the everyday lyric of a common scene.

Joshua C. Taylor

BALLA: *Dynamism of a Dog on a Leash.* 1912.

Oil on canvas, 35⅜" x 43¼". Albright-Knox Art Gallery, Buffalo. Courtesy of George F. Goodyear and The Buffalo Fine Arts Academy

BY 1910 Léger had commenced his involvement with Cubism and with pictorial compositions that "manipulate form for form's sake." He referred to his new style as "multiplicative painting"—an abstract method which brought about a period of pictorial liberation.

The key concept of Léger's new method, seen in *Woman in an Armchair*, was that of heightened contrast. Swiftly curving forms were violently juxtaposed with jagged, angular ones; quickly brushed patches of color were broken by the brilliant white of highlights or exposed canvas. The contrasts were intensified by repetition throughout the canvas, splaying out the geometric forms in syncopated patterns. The seated figure, divested of all sensuous, indeed human, appeal, became a kaleidoscope of quasi-mechanical forms.

However, instead of the transparent, fractured planes of the Cubists, Léger's pictorial vocabulary consisted of volumetric cones and cylinders, locked into place with architectonic rigor. In Katharine Kuh's words, "His approach is more direct, his emphasis on construction." Léger himself said, "I build, I am a Norman."

The dynamism of Léger's compositions also reached beyond Cubism and Futurism. Here the abstract forms of the figure became a rotating spiral emanating from the central axis of the head, the segmented arms initiating circular rhythms which are emphasized by the dashing linear and color patterns. Yet Léger believed that the most ordinary, static subject could convey the excitement and dynamism of machines, that it was not necessary, as the Futurists had done, to seek out actual mechanical subjects.

And the many such studies of seated figures of 1912–13 prove him right. Each version, through subtle variations in the articulation of the arms, the tilt of the head, the architectural tension of the whole, attests to the consistent excellence of the solutions that Léger reached in working out the pictorial problems he posed for himself.

Susana Leval

LEGER: *Woman in an Armchair.* 1912.

Oil on canvas, 51⅜ x 38⅜".
Lydia and Harry Lewis Winston Collection (Dr. and Mrs. Barnett Malbin, New York)

WHEN THIS canvas, alternatively titled *Knife Grinder*, was exhibited in 1913 in Moscow, Malevich was calling his work "Cubo-Futurist." The prismatic forms are in a general way Cubistic; the repeated, overlapping shapes of foot, hands, and scissor blades recall the Futurist formula for expressing movement. Marcel Duchamp's *Nude Descending the Staircase* was painted in the same year. Malevich's forms, however, unlike those of Duchamp, are brightly colored; like Léger's, they seem to be made of metal sheets and cylinders. But Malevich, like the Russian Futurist poets of his generation, saw in the machine not so much the glorification of power and movement as such—the basic aim of the Italians—as a celebration of Russia's emerging and socially challenging industrial society. Malevich himself, as George Heard Hamilton has written, "always insisted on the ethical and philosophical values of his art." This seems to have been true even after 1914, when he turned from his early style, so well illustrated in the *Scissors Grinder*, to the pure abstraction of Suprematism ("the supremacy of feeling in creative art") which he proclaimed in 1914. Feeling was not to be aroused through association with recognizable objects or situations, but by the direct experience of color and proportion in absolute purity. In this he is related to Mondrian, the later Kandinsky, and El Lissitzky, whom he strongly influenced.

Born in Kiev, Malevich taught at the First Free State School of Arts and Crafts in Moscow, and later at the Museum of Artistic Culture in Petrograd (now Leningrad). As a Christian mystic, he saw his art as a vehicle for the expression of antimaterialistic ideals; even when, later in his career, he turned to architecture, the theater, and industrial design, he never had so utilitarian an approach as did many who, like some of the Bauhaus group, came so profitably under his influence.

Katherine B. Neilson

MALEVICH: *Scissors Grinder.*
1912.
Oil on canvas, 31⅜ x 31⅜".
Yale University Art Gallery,
New Haven.
Gift of Collection Société Anonyme

IN THIS exhibition, *Scissors Grinder* has been lent from the collection of the Société Anonyme, founded in 1920 by Katherine S. Dreier, an American painter. In addition to assembling an extraordinary collection of modern art, the Société Anonyme presented exhibitions and held special events. Miss Dreier's chief collaborator was Marcel Duchamp. In 1941, the collection was given to Yale University. Fernand Léger's painting *People in a Garden*, in this exhibition (page 239), formerly belonged to that collection.

W.S.L.

"AS A SPANIARD," Gertrude Stein wrote of Juan Gris, "he knew Cubism and had stepped through into it." It would be a mistake, nevertheless, to assume that he stepped into Cubism all at once and without a single backward glance. In 1911 Gris had worked his way cautiously through Post-Impressionism and on to a qualified but increasingly Cubist definition of form. In 1912 he gradually evolved a personal style and, as Braque and Picasso had done before him, began to include lettering in his compositions.

In 1912 Gris painted the *Man in a Café* for which at least three preparatory drawings exist. Remembering hearsay accounts of Gris's solemnity of mind, one wonders how deliberate was the picture's almost comic spirit. The complacent man with absurdly high heels seems a caricature of the member of the bourgeoisie, arrived to take his ease at a sidewalk café, staring straight ahead at the passers-by. Even the distortions of the man's face are witty, whether intentionally so or not, and at this point, perhaps assured of his growing mastery as an artist, Gris may well have worked in a more relaxed, even playful spirit.

The *Man in a Café*, like the *Smoker* of the succeeding year, is gay in temper and helps qualify the impression of Gris's unyielding solemnity of which some of his friends have spoken. Considering the affection with which Gris was regarded by those closest to him, considering even such characteristics as his love of dancing, often mentioned in his letters, he cannot have been a cold personality.

James Thrall Soby

GRIS: *Man in a Café.* 1912.
Oil on canvas, 50⅝ x 34⅝".
Philadelphia Museum of Art.
The Louise and Walter Arensberg
Collection

ANOTHER of Gris's masterworks of 1913 is the *Still Life with Pears*, in which we can easily recognize what was to become an earmark of Gris's art—the echoed application of comparable shapes to objects of differing character and identity within a given composition. In Douglas Cooper's words, "One finds, for example, the same oval form used in a single canvas to express the beak of a flute, the sphere of a glass, the neck of a bottle, the rose of a guitar, and a bunch of grapes in a fruit bowl." Thus in the *Still Life with Pears* the round profile of a glass is played against the top of a second glass seen from a contrasting angle (that is, from above); both forms are repeated in the foreground's cluster of grapes. Rose and blue cloths or draperies contrast with the marbleized brown of the table on which the dark pears and grapes are placed; they contrast even more violently with the almost Oriental yellow of the newspaper— obviously *Le Matin*, from the Victorian lettering of the word "Le"—the straw caning of the chair and the buff-orange of its wooden back.

By this time Gris has become the original colorist he was to remain throughout the remainder of his short career. Indeed, his color is one of his most inimitable gifts, unpredictable to extreme degree, variable and running the gamut from luxury to terse sobriety. Possibly one reason why Gris's fame for a long time lagged behind that of his greatest colleagues in Cubism is the fact that his paintings' qualities are often lost in the black-and-white reproductions which served to spread the fame of Picasso and Braque. This is not to claim that he was a finer colorist than they; it is to assert that his color is unusually elusive and hard to hold accurately in memory, so that only through a careful study of his paintings themselves can one arrive at anything like a fair estimate of his worth.

James Thrall Soby

GRIS: *Still Life with Pears.* 1913.

Oil on canvas, 21¼ x 28¾". Collection Mr. and Mrs. Burton Tremaine, Meriden, Conn.

IN AUGUST 1913, Gris and his wife, Josette, joined Picasso at Céret near the Spanish border. They remained until November. This was the first time Gris had left Paris since his arrival in 1906. He was delighted by the change and perhaps also, despite his persistent disclaimers of any interest in his native land, by his proximity to Spain. At any rate, during his months at Céret he worked superbly, producing such works as the *Violin and Guitar*, which he described in a letter to D.-H. Kahnweiler, his dealer and lifelong champion, as his own favorite.

Though Gris's contribution to Analytical Cubism had been his own and admirable, there can be no doubt that he welcomed the technical and stylistic expansion which Synthetic Cubism allowed him. *Violin and Guitar* is daring in color. But its pyramidal maze of forms based on musical instruments is compelling. Indeed, the taut, elegant, and inevitable contours of the violin had more persistent meaning for Gris than for his fellow Cubists. It is true that Braque also had been fascinated by violins and had accentuated their keys, scrolls, and sound holes in a number of works, among them the *Piano and Mandola* and the *Violin and Palette* of 1909-10 (page 141). Picasso made more frequent use of the guitar and mandolin, whose rounded outlines better suited his purpose. There has been a considerable amount of theorizing as to why musical instruments meant so much to the Cubists in general, and the musical inclinations of Picasso, Braque, Gris, and the others have perhaps been overstressed. It seems more plausible to assume that the Cubists, in their arduous task of reappraising everyday appearances through a new and revolutionary plastic system, liked the violin, the guitar, and the mandolin because the basic design of these instruments had undergone very little change for several centuries. Their challenge to the Cubists was therefore all the more explicit. At any rate, the violin's complexity of design appears in a sense to symbolize the conscientious intellectuality which Gris brought to Cubist research. This is not to say, of course, that he was more intellectual than his two great colleagues. But he was, one assumes, more metaphysical in his conception of how the commonplace and the traditional could become the point of departure for a new order in painting.

James Thrall Soby

GRIS: *Violin and Guitar*. 1913.
Oil on canvas, 39⅝ x 25⅞".
Collection Mr. and Mrs.
Ralph F. Colin, New York.
See color plate, page 26

ANALYTIC CUBISM was in no sense a movement. It had been a stylistic marriage of two painters, and it had concerned only them.

In structuring their compositions, Braque and Picasso jettisoned color. Their method of depicting what they saw became increasingly refined, even abstruse, so that the actual content of their painting was difficult to comprehend. How much further could Analytic Cubism go? An ultimate decision (and one taken by Kupka and Malevich) might have been to change the theory of their painting, which was representation, and choose instead abstraction. Such a step neither Braque nor Picasso was willing to take. Each sought alternate, individually different, roads.

Throughout his career Picasso explored successive styles which he very often left to others to dilute. He was, however, incapable of repeating himself, unless inherent in the subject was a theme which had possibilities of continuous narrative, or unless the subject, in its very depiction, offered a variety of pictorial solutions.

A certain whimsy had already infiltrated Picasso's painting in 1913. The following summer in Avignon, he allowed it free reign. A series of drawings of female nudes, often quite mad, alternates with studies after Cézanne. The young girl at the left, however, has little resemblance to any seated figure by the master of Aix, although her curiously fisted hands do directly derive from a study of specific paintings by him. At any rate, the young lady appears magnificently giddy in her festooned hat and boa. And did Picasso intend a parody of a portrait by Matisse painted in the previous year with the same insistent green?

The arrangements of the figure and the objects is free, for instance the light bulb (in Avignon a novelty in 1914) by her arm. The forms are also more defined and thus more readable than in Analytic Cubism. The wide range of colors against the pervasive background color is completely alien to the sobriety of previous years. In addition, Picasso mixed sand with his paint and further enlivened the surface with concentrated areas of Pointillist dots. What is most interesting, perhaps, is how Picasso actually evolved the picture. Without paper or paste he has painted a collage. This was, indeed, his method. The floral patterns were cut from commercial wallpaper and then simulated in paint. The girl's hands and her boa were drawn on separate sheets, as was the light bulb, then cut and arranged flat so that Picasso could copy them. Last, the fruit bowl with grapes imitates a still-life drawing of the period.

W.S.L.

PICASSO:
Portrait of a Young Girl. 1914.
Oil on canvas, 51¼ x 38¼".
Musée National d'Art Moderne,
Paris.
Bequest of Georges Salles.
See color plate, page 27

IN THE autumn of 1887, Lyonel Feininger sailed for Germany and docked at Hamburg. He would not return to the United States for half a century. His first visit to Paris, in 1892, was brief. In 1906 and 1907, however, he spent twenty months in the French capital. He returned in 1911 and wrote to his wife, Julia, who remained in Germany, in Bonn: "Where am I to begin telling about all that has happened? Experiences follow one upon the other so rapidly that the new ones almost blot out the older, and I am exultant constantly . . . It has been a wonderful time. For me it means an end and a new beginning out of the wealth of new experiences, with no more brooding or tormenting doubts."

W.S.L.

FEININGER: *Alley of Trees.* 1914.

Oil on canvas, 31¾ x 39¾".
Private collection, New York.
See color plate, page 25

IN THE spring of 1911, Feininger found the Parisian art world "agog with Cubism." The highly abstract works of Braque and Picasso, with whom he exhibited at the Salon des Indépendants, were revelations to Feininger. Yet he found their work peculiarly consonant with the spirit of his own, intuitively arrived at pictorial researches.

From then on, Feininger remained abreast with the artistic avant-garde. In Berlin in 1912, he established contact with members of The Bridge (who had moved there from Dresden) and also saw Futurist works. The following year, at the invitation of Franz Marc, he exhibited with The Blue Rider group in Munich.

The vocabulary of Cubism is evident in this fascinating picture, with its translucent, interpenetrating planes and suffocatingly shallow space. Yet Feininger's aim was far different from the Cubists': "They pluck to pieces, and I strain in the opposite direction—concentration, monumentality." Instead of fracturing and dislocating the object, his jagged planes lock together irrevocably to form a coherent image. Here too, color, nonexistent in Cubism, assumes a cohesive role.

The Futurist tension and energy of this image also deny the classical stasis of the Cubist perception. Unbearably compressed diagonals energize every inch of the canvas, initiating moving rhythms, rejecting the perpendicular infrastructure of Cubism. Undoubtedly, Feininger was influenced by the dynamic Futurist concept of "lines of force" present in all phenomena. The sense of conflict and unrest is heightened by the shifting scale between the dwarfed walking figure and the towering trees.

Susana Leval

FRANZ MARC, like Feininger, underwent in 1911–14 a double apprenticeship to Cubism and Futurism. Like Feininger also, he assimilated what he learned into a uniquely personal, romantic vision.

Marc's romanticism was expressed in a particular sensitivity to the animal world. Horses, deer, gazelles, bulls, wild beasts—all for him were pure beings, at one with the secret forces of nature and from whom man could learn. "The still virgin sense of life possessed by animals awoke in me all that is noblest." Marc depicted animals in mystic communion with primal nature, unspoiled by man. Seeking to reveal their hidden spiritual life, he interpreted natural phenomena as reflections of the feelings of animals. In his more somber visions, the creatures seem threatened by the cataclysmic forces created by man's destruction of nature's harmonious balance.

MARC: *Animals in a Landscape.*
1914.

Oil on canvas, 43⅜ x 39¼".
The Detroit Institute of Arts.
Gift of Robert Hudson Tannahill

Marc's particular sensitivity is yet another expression of the search, so prevalent during the second decade of this century, for a "pure" art of spiritual values which would penetrate to the immaterial core of the visible world. It was precisely on these grounds that Kandinsky and Marc founded the Blue Rider in 1911 (page 118).

Since 1905, Marc had been executing exquisitely detailed, naturalistic studies of animals in a style which betrayed first Art Nouveau, then Impressionist, influences. In 1910, through contact with the Fauves and Kandinsky, he used color with increasing freedom, incorporating the juxtaposition of complementaries. The year 1912 brought contact with the Futurists in Munich and with Delaunay in Paris, and the final crystallization of Marc's mature style, of which this painting is such an eloquent example.

Marc's brilliant use of color has gone beyond the use of complementaries to the intensity of Delaunay's dissonant harmonies. The jagged, angular rhythms recall the turbulent dynamism of Futurist and Rayonnist compositions. In this painting, the outlines of three animals can barely be discerned within the maelstrom of linear and colored rhythms. One cow, at the upper left, rests peacefully in an embryonic position; the other merges with the vegetation upon which it gently grazes. The male, the horned bull, stands in the center of the composition.

Susana Leval

"VIOLENT CONTRASTS of patches of color, women's clothes, vivid shawls of exquisite and metallic greens, and watermelons. Colored shapes: women disappearing behind mountains of pumpkins, vegetables, in fairyland markets." Thus did Delaunay describe the spectacle of Portuguese life which he so brilliantly recaptures in this picture. The intense Iberian light had dazzled him, and it led his researches in color to extremely vivid harmonies.

As early as 1912, with the geometrically abstract color mosaics of the *Windows on the City* series, Delaunay had been painting pictures whose very subject was color and whose lyrical dynamism prompted musical analogies—the poet Guillaume Apollinaire gave the style the name "Orphism." Yet, like Seurat and the Neo-Impressionists, Delaunay had sought in the work of M. E. Chevreul a scientific basis for his color research.

The Sideboard, entitled in French *La Verseuse* or *Nature Morte Portugaise*, is a brilliant achievement of harmonious contrast. The entire canvas is energized by vibrations, physically perceptible to the eye, of simultaneous color contrasts—Delaunay's ideal "movement." As Gilles de la Tourette has pointed out, there is a masterful combination of slow vibrations (by the juxtaposition of complementaries) and of very rapid ones (by the juxtaposition of dissonant colors). The gray tablecloth and the delicate pastel tones at the top of the picture scrupulously follow Chevreul's suggestions as devices to heighten neighboring colors.

This painting, as well as an almost identical version in the collection of Louis Carré, is also an extraordinarily daring display of alternations between representational and abstract painting. The table's angle, cast shadows, carefully painted garment ornamentation, highlights on cloth—all these lend classic naturalism, depth, and stability to the picture. And then, in hallucinatory fashion, the lusciously heaped lemons, oranges, and watermelons become iridescent orbs that float to the picture's edge. The final tour de force is the woman's face, a completely abstract, emblematic disk which simultaneously looks back to Delaunay's original "disk" of 1912 and forward to his breathtaking series of *Rhythms* painted in the final years.

Susana Leval

DELAUNAY: *The Sideboard.*
1916.
Oil and encaustic on canvas,
55⅛ x 59½".
Musée National d'Art Moderne, Paris

IN MAY OF 1915, war became a reality for the Italians, and those able among the Futurists were with the first to volunteer. In July, Boccioni, Luigi Russolo, Antonio Sant'Elia, Filippo Tommaso Marinetti, and many younger associates became members of the volunteer cyclists. Mario Sironi was already at the front.

In Paris, which he had reached late in 1914, ill and in desperate financial circumstances, Severini continued to respond to the war in his own way, creating a series of drawings and paintings that bristle with the harsh lines and mechanical patterns of military matériel. As with the others, his interest in purely abstract suggestion waned. Yet in spite of the grim nature of the subject matter, Severini found a fresh, clean beauty in such unlikely objects as the *Armored Train*. He found new beauty also in the airplane, not because it was the symbol of speed, as it appealed to Marinetti and Balla, but because it afforded—actually and to the imagination—a new kaleidoscopic view of the earth. Many of these works were brought together for an exhibition in Paris in January 1916, which Severini boldly advertised as the "First Futurist Exhibition of Plastic Art of the War." Severini's active adherence to Futurism, however, was almost at an end.

Joshua C. Taylor

SEEN FROM above and appearing vertically is an open, armored train which serves as a moving trench for five hooded soldiers who set their rifles on the metal facing and aim to the left. At the end of the car, a revolving cannon shoots in the same direction. Smoke and gunfire billow from the machine of war.

From his apartment at Igny, a suburb of Paris, Severini could see the tracks on which military and civilian trains rolled in and out of Paris. In 1959, Severini wrote that he had also been inspired by photographs of trains which were published in contemporary newspapers and magazines. When asked whether or not the subject had any special significance, Severini must have been startled at the naïveté of the question. He answered, however, "It is the witness of a technology invented to destroy and not to construct."

The Museum of Modern Art owns a preparatory drawing, in charcoal, close to this tight and rigid composition. The drawing, however, lacks the sharp, crystalline qualities of the painting. On its verso, in the artist's hand, appears in French and in Italian the more specific title "Armored Train in Action." The painting is a pendant to a slightly earlier picture, *The Train of the Wounded*, identical in view, format, and dimensions, which is owned by the Stedelijk Museum in Amsterdam.

W.S.L.

SEVERINI: *Armored Train in Action.* 1915.
Oil on canvas, 46 x 34½".
Collection Richard S. Zeisler, New York

ABSTRACT ART in Russia began long before the Revolution of 1917. The succession of artistic movements of the years 1917–22 was merely a continuation of the previous five years' excitement in which Cubism, Rayonism, Suprematism, Non-Objectivism, Cubo-Futurism, and Constructivism had been born and, in some cases, had died. The Suprematist–Non-Objectivist movement was by far the most important development for Russian abstract painting.

It was inevitable that the impulse toward pure abstraction should have been carried to an absolute conclusion sooner or later. In Munich, Kandinsky is held to have painted a pure abstraction as early as 1911. But as may be seen in the 1913 *Little Pleasures* (page 121), Kandinsky's spontaneous rather than amorphous forms frequently if unintentionally assumed the shapes of recognizable objects. In other words, his method was not proof against impurity.

The first artist to establish a system of absolutely pure geometrical abstract composition was the Russo-Polish painter Kasimir Malevich of Moscow. In 1911–12 he had developed a Cubist formula related to, but apparently independent of, the work of Léger and Duchamp during those years. His *Scissors Grinder* of 1912 (page 155) is definitely more advanced than Léger at the same time. Malevich suddenly foresaw the logical and inevitable conclusion toward which European art was moving: "In the year 1913, in my desperate struggle to free art from the ballast of the objective world, I fled to the form of the Square and exhibited a picture which was nothing more or less than a black square upon a white background. The critics moaned and with them the public: 'Everything we loved is lost: We are in a desert . . . Before us stands a black square on a white ground.' "

In the history of abstract art Malevich is a figure of fundamental importance. As a pioneer, a theorist, and an artist he influenced not only a large following in Russia but also, through Lissitzky and Moholy-Nagy, the course of abstract art in Central Europe. He stands at the heart of the movement which swept westward from Russia after World War I and, mingling with the eastward moving influence of the Dutch de Stijl group, transformed the architecture, furniture, typography, and commercial art of Germany and much of the rest of Europe.

Alfred H. Barr, Jr.

MALEVICH: *Dynamic Suprematism.* 1916.

Oil on canvas, 40¼ x 26¼".
Collection Dr. Armand Hammer, Los Angeles

THE PAINTED DREAM

THREE YEARS after his death, Guillaume Apollinaire wrote of Rousseau: "The douanier went to the very end in his work, something very rare today. His paintings were made without method, system, or mannerisms. From this comes the variety in his work. He did not distrust his imagination any more than he did his hand. From this comes the grace and richness of his decorative compositions. He had taken part in the Mexican campaign, and his poetic and plastic recollections of tropical vegetation and fauna were most precise. The result has been that this Breton, this old man who lived mostly in the suburbs of Paris, is without doubt the most extraordinary, the boldest, the most charming painter of the exotic . . . But Rousseau was more than a decorator; he was not just an image-maker; he was a painter. It is this which makes comprehension of his work so difficult for some people. He had a feeling for order, as is shown, not only in his pictures, but also in his drawings, which are as ordered as Persian miniatures. His art had purity, as is shown in his feminine figures, in the structure of his trees, and the harmonious song of the different tones of a single color."

Although Rousseau did serve in the French army, as a member of a military band, during the years when an expeditionary force was engaged in the unfortunate venture that led to the short-lived Mexican Empire, there is every reason to believe that he never left France. But the fact that he did not see any tropical vegetation except in the Paris botanical gardens does not of course detract from the haunting qualities of his exotic paintings.

We also know that Rousseau's tropical vegetation and fauna, far from being based on "plastic recollections,"are actually the product of his fertile imagination. But where is the harm? The Occident, which has always liked to dream of exotic paradises, readily accepted the enchanting world invented by Gauguin. The one represented by Rousseau is just as "real." It is characterized by luscious colors and neatly assembled forms, by exquisite shapes of blossoms, leaves, branches, or foliage which, repeated throughout his compositions, create rhythms of great beauty, suggesting luxuriant plant life. There is no trace of the clumsy draftsmanship which lends so many of Rousseau's works their awkward and naïve charm. In tropical landscapes such as this, the painter, liberated from the necessity or the desire for verisimilitude, followed his inspiration to reach truth on a higher level, the truth of grandiose dreams which artistic realization endows with a new reality.

John Rewald

ROUSSEAU: *The Merry Jesters.*
c. 1906.

Oil on canvas, 57⅜ x 44⅝".
Philadelphia Museum of Art.
The Louise and Walter Arensberg
Collection.
See color plate, page 30

REDON WAS greatly admired by the Symbolist poets in France and Belgium, who saw in his graphic work a visual complement to their own writings. Stéphane Mallarmé wrote of Redon: "In our silences you ruffle the plumage of reverie and night . . . What is personal in you issues from your dreams. Demonic lithographer, your invention is as profound as certain of your blacks!" The Symbolist critic and translator of Poe, Emil Hennequin, suggested to Redon that he read Flaubert's *The Temptation of Saint Anthony*. "You will find new monsters," Hennequin said, and indeed in this image-studded drama Redon discovered his greatest literary inspiration. In three different series of illustrations, together his most ambitious graphic work, he gave visual form to Flaubert's text.

For twenty years, Redon had worked almost exclusively on paper and in black and white. After 1900, he abandoned lithography (except for a few portraits of friends) and turned to color, painting and drawing in vivid and intense hues. With the exception of the brilliantly colored flower pieces for which he is best known, many of the pastels and paintings rework earlier themes. The composition of the painting *Death* is after an 1889 lithograph to Flaubert. Death, a mythic demigod from an obscure netherworld, announces, "mine irony surpasses that of all others."

In the original image, in the lithograph, the protagonist is clearly a woman. Uncoiled, she stands in a chiaroscuro light, her face partially hidden by her hair which sinuously swirls across the top of the composition. Here, the figure has become a man, a startling apparition painted green. There is torment rather than enchantment in his reverie.

The picture is brilliantly colored and, instead of hair, a yellow cumulous mass floats at the top. Working in oil, Redon was attracted by the various possible textures and contrasts of paint itself. Often, on the same canvas, he combined smoothly applied strokes with a heavy impasto. Here, in the lower right corner, the staccatolike application of colors is a dazzling tour de force.

Of a younger generation of painters it was perhaps Matisse who most appreciated the lesson of Redon's color. The Surrealists were more influenced by his visions, and in his beliefs they found a precursor. "My originality consists in putting the logic of the visible to the service of the invisible," he had written. "I create imaginary beings in terms of material logic."

W.S.L.

REDON: *Death.* After 1905.
Oil on cardboard, 22⅜ x 18¾".
Collection Mrs. Bertram Smith,
New York

WITNESSING the rise of new aesthetics, in contact with the different expressions of the "heroic" period in the early part of the twentieth century, de Chirico found himself in 1912 confronted with the problem of following one of the roads already opened or of opening a new road. He avoided Fauvism as well as Cubism and introduced what could be called "metaphysical painting." Instead of exploiting the coming medium of abstraction, he organized on his canvases the meeting of elements which could only meet in a "metaphysical world." These elements, painted in the minutest technique, were "exposed" on a horizontal plane in orthodox perspective. This technique, in opposition to the Cubist or purely abstract formula in full bloom at that moment, protected de Chirico's position and allowed him to lay down the foundation of what was to become Surrealism ten years later.

Marcel Duchamp

DE CHIRICO: *The Evil Genius of a King.* 1914–15.
Oil on canvas, 24 x 19¾".
The Museum of Modern Art, New York

BETWEEN 1910 and 1915, when he lived in Paris, de Chirico composed a series of still lifes in which disparate, often incongruous objects are situated in architectural settings. These paintings, their titles and architecture sometimes evoke a nostalgia for his native Italy.

When looking at de Chirico's painting the eye is compelled to travel upward. One sees first the flat receding plane, rising abruptly, upon which a "still life" has been arranged. But who placed these objects, what is their significance, will they remain? Are these, indeed, the toys of a prince? Some are thought to be remembrances from childhood—a ball, a paper hat, perhaps favors from a party. Others are more curious, their appearance enigmatic, indeed ominous—for instance the cannon.

The vanishing points of almost all forms and architectural elements radically differ. These changing perspectives, however, are unified by the intense light emanating from the right. De Chirico follows the dictates of subconscious association rather than those of logic or custom. The disquieting result invites Freudian analysis.

De Chirico was not only the immediate and the most important forerunner of Surrealism, he also restored to contemporary painting the use of deep perspective. His portrayals of receding planes and his scaling of objects were adopted by such Surrealist painters as Delvaux and Tanguy (pages 195, 197). *The Evil Genius of a King* might be contrasted with the hallucinatory and inflated images of Magritte painted almost forty years later (page 199). De Chirico conveys a feeling of premonition. Magritte a sense of astonishment.

W.S.L.

CHAGALL is a conscious artist. While the selection and combination of his images may appear illogical from a representational viewpoint, they are carefully and rationally chosen elements for the pictorial structure he seeks to build. There is nothing automatic in his work. In fact his much talked of illogicality appears only when his paintings are read detail by detail; taken in the composite they have the same pictorial integrity as the most naturalistic painting, or the most architectural Cubist work of the same level of quality. He is an artist with a full color sense. He has a deep regard for technique. He is a subtle craftsman who, rather than dull his hand in virtuosity, affects clumsiness. He is an artist who has been content with a limited repertory of representational forms. But his work of nearly an astonishing seventy years shows a persistent effort to bring out new and richer effects from his consciously limited thematic material by unaccustomed arrangements and by a steady development of a more complex technique. In an age that has fled from sentiment he has drawn constantly on it for stimulation. And our debt to Chagall is to an artist who has brought poetry back into painting through subject matter, without any sacrifice of his painter's interest in the picture for itself, and entirely aside from any communication that can be put into words.

James Johnson Sweeney

CHAGALL: *Birthday.* 1915.
Oil on cardboard, 31¾ x 39¼".
The Museum of Modern Art, New York.
Acquired through the Lillie P. Bliss
Bequest.
See color plate, page 29

DURING World War I, Chagall returned to Russia. On his birthday in 1915, shortly before their marriage, his fiancée presented him a bouquet. In her autobiography, Bella recalled their rapture: "Soon I forget the flowers. You work with your brushes . . . Your canvas quivers . . . You pour on color . . . Suddenly . . . you jump into the air . . . You float among the rafters. You turn your head and you twist mine too . . . and both together we rise over the clean little room . . . 'How do you like my picture?' you ask . . . You wait and are afraid of what I may tell you. It's very good . . . you float away so beautifully. We'll call it the birthday."

Chagall presented to The Museum of Modern Art a preliminary and scaled drawing for the painting. The drawing is dated July 7, the artist's twenty-eighth birthday. The painting was first exhibited in Moscow in 1916 and subsequently in Berlin. When it was shown in Paris in 1923, it was greatly admired by the art dealer Paul Guillaume, who commissioned a replica now owned by The Solomon R. Guggenheim Museum.

W.S.L.

THE WOMAN'S head is represented by a simple black shape crowned with hair radiating from it, but otherwise the symbols clearly defined on a pale blue background are more cryptic. The body of the mother is condensed into a black conical shape pierced by a round hole. It appears to swing like a pendulum hung by a thin straight line from the head, while two small embryonic creatures, potentially human, climb toward shapes which we recognize as the woman's breasts. One breast is seen in profile and the other as a circle which could also be an eye or even the sun. Between them a shape, fish or spermatozoon, swims through the all-enveloping ether. There is an obvious resemblance between these small eager creatures and parasites that cling like children for food and protection to a parent body.

This picture is of interest because it demonstrates a development in Miró's use of symbols. Renouncing the diversity of images and detail with which he had enjoyed enriching earlier paintings, here he uses signs with strict economy and places them in a significant relation to each other. They are so linked and move so inevitably together that they have an organic unity, becoming a single anatomy that floats in a clear luminous element. This complex taken as a whole produces a new visual image of maternity which evokes in us deep reactions and a wealth of associations. It brings with it the conviction that we are approaching a new or perhaps very primitive sense of reality.

Roland Penrose

MIRO: *Maternity*. 1924.
Oil on canvas, 36⅝ x 28¾".
Private collection, London

MIRO'S *Painting* is composed of abstract biomorphic forms. Though it was actually developed from a collage made in the same year, in which Miró had pasted onto a sheet of paper nine halftone illustrations of machinery, he characteristically metamorphosed the mechanical shapes so that they seem to refer in highly schematized fashion to animals, such as horned cattle. All the elements except the one at the upper left, which is shaded and highlighted in a manner that suggests three dimensions, are evenly painted in black, white, or red, or rendered simply in outline. The device of changing the tone of a shape as it intersects another one appears frequently in Miró's work from about this time on. He seems to have adopted it as a convention to imply, within his overall two-dimensional scheme, that the shapes should be thought of as occupying different planes.

The biomorphic forms in the *Painting* float against a luminous, atmospheric background divided into geometrical fields of color. The smoky tones and blurred edges of these areas are somewhat unusual for Miró, who in general prefers bright colors and crisp outlines. The large size of the canvas and its resulting monumental effect are also rather exceptional in his work, though in the following year he produced a series of big pictures intended to serve as designs for tapestries, and later in his career he created murals and large-scale ceramics to be placed in architectural settings.

Helen M. Franc

MIRO: *Painting*. 1933.
Oil on canvas, 68½ x 77¼".
The Museum of Modern Art, New York.
Gift of the Advisory Committee

IN AN AGE that blasted privacy Paul Klee built a small but exquisite shrine to intimacy.

Klee did not belong to the tradition of the great decorators. Though he derived from the German Expressionist school that stemmed out of van Gogh and Munch, he was a designer in feathers rather than in flame. In an age that felt "it was necessary to shake an adult to get a reaction out of him," Klee lived fully in elaborating nuances and capturing fancies. He was not a painter whose work speaks to us from a distance. Klee was fundamentally a cabinet artist who should be read and reread, in a manner of speaking, on the knee. The subtle complexity of his texture justifies it. He spoke in a mixed tongue of representational and technical fantasy. These were fused by a remarkably untrammeled sensibility. The result was a curious pictorial poetry all his own. And in this character of so much of Klee's work we often feel a closer affinity with Oriental art than with that of the Occident.

Yet if Klee did not belong to the tradition of the great Western decorators, he was the product of a tradition that has deeply marked our times. Klee was born in 1879. Consequently his early impressionable years fell within the nineties—in Central Europe the decade of Munch and Ferdinand Hodler, of Henri van de Velde and Hermann Obrist, and particularly of the Art Nouveau-Jugendstil movement. The keynote of the painting of this period was a stress on the basic linear pattern of an expression. Behind it lay the discovery of the Japanese print in the middle of the nineteenth century and, more recently, the adaptation of the Japanese print's broad, running contour lines by Gauguin, van Gogh, and their Synthetist followers. Out of it came a new recognition of the immediacy and intimacy with which the emotions speak through the hand when it is not too closely controlled by the conscious, reasoning mind.

During the decade following 1905 we see traces of other, newer influences: Matisse, Alfred Kubin, Nolde, the new German interest in children's drawings, Kandinsky, Delaunay, and the Paris Cubists in general. Finally, about 1917, Klee's early bent began to reassert itself: "fantasy expressed in predominantly linear compositions"—a calligraphic expression sensitive to the most delicate suggestions of the nervous system, responsive to the most subtle unconscious associations. This was the Klee whom the Surrealists recognized as a precursor: a precursor in just such expressions of free sensibility as they ambitioned to achieve: an explorer of intimate lyric rhythms, who never felt the need to undertake Surrealism's destructive work before concentrating on the problems raised in art by the "discovery" of the unconscious. This was the Klee who was to persevere in scrupulous craftsmanship and yet grow in invention, lightness of touch, and richness of texture until his death in 1940.

James Johnson Sweeney

KLEE: *Man with Top Hat.* 1925.
Gouache, pen and ink on paper,
15⅛ x 10⅝".
Private collection, New York

KLEE: *Portal of a Mosque.* 1931.
Watercolor on paper, 14¾ x 11½".
Collection Mr. and Mrs. Ralph F. Colin,
New York

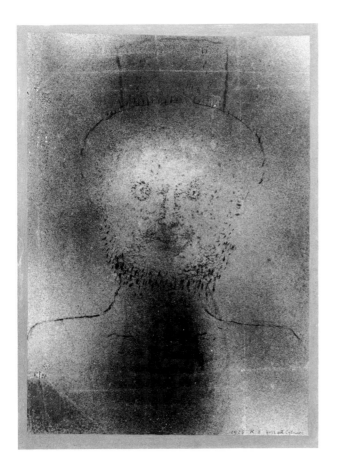

IN 1904 Klee worked on a series of etchings several of which are allegoric, sometimes with classical allusions. One of them, *Woman and Deer*, is perhaps Klee's first reference to the legend of Diana. When studied, however, the image of the Olympian deity with a stag assumes implications not traditionally associated with the goddess of chastity.

In a few brightly colored watercolors of 1927, Klee experimented briefly with a Divisionist technique. He spent the summer on the islands of Porquerolles and Corsica. Perhaps the shimmering, sun-drenched colors of the Mediterranean had the same effect upon Klee as they had earlier upon Signac and Matisse.

Between 1930 and 1932, Klee further developed his Divisionist technique not only in watercolor but in oil. During this period, he worked concurrently in at least two other styles. The assigned problem of the Divisionist pictures is the representation of light, intense and pulsating. In the *Diana*, however, the shades are darker as befits the goddess of the moon and night.

Klee was anxious that his Divisionist technique—lyric, although he called it "crops of dots"—not be confused with the scientific method of the Neo-Impressionist painter Seurat. It is impossible, however, not to compare the techniques of both artists, and, in this exhibition, other adaptations of Pointillism can be studied in paintings by Derain, Picasso, and Signac (pages 71, 113, 163).

Diana, one of Klee's largest oils, is also one of the most beautiful. Each "dot" is placed precisely, and the juxtapositions of blue and its two complementary colors are as delicate as they are sure. The hieroglyph of *Diana* is posed against the sky. She is clad in a tunic and wears a cape. She stands on a wheel, an allusion to her chariot drawn by stags. As in a later watercolor entitled *Diana in the Autumn Wind*, her garments billow in a breeze. Her head, the focus of the picture, is partially concealed. The wrapped figure suggests, inescapably, that celestial temperatures might be chill. She is portrayed as Diana, the huntress. Above her brow is not the crescent moon but another attribute, the quivered arrow which points in the direction toward which she moves.

W.S.L.

KLEE: *Diana*. 1931.
Oil on canvas, 31½ x 23¾".
Collection Mrs. William A. Bernoudy,
St. Louis

IN THE HUGE picture *The Mountain*, Balthus has challenged Courbet on a grand scale. The parallel is with the almost equally large painting by Courbet called *The Young Ladies of the Village*, in the Metropolitan Museum of Art, New York. Painted in 1851, this allies a landscape with which Courbet was intimately familiar with people no less well known to him: his three sisters. *The Mountain*, painted in 1937, has these same characteristics: a landscape which Balthus had known since boyhood, figurants drawn from himself and the people nearest to him. In his treatment of landscape on a large scale, Courbet proceeded throughout with a post-Romantic heaviness and literalness which was not quite Balthus' way. The landscape in *The Mountain* has a crystalline quality which is, on the contrary, pre-Romantic: a message from the world of Carl Gustav Carus and Caspar David Friedrich. The figures, too, have a note of undergraduate high spirits, as if young people with a superabundance of energy had set off with the equipment prescribed by Baedeker (" a light game-bag or *gibecière*," for instance) and were acting out all the absurdities that came into their heads: hallooing, shamming sleep, striking the attitudes prescribed by Victorian tradition, and yet being genuinely carried away by the grandeur of the scene and the pleasure of one another's company.

La Montagne is to Balthus what *Bonjour, M. Courbet* was to Courbet: a major work full of private allusions and permeated by powerful feelings about particular people in a particular landscape.

John Russell

BALTHUS: *The Mountain*. 1937.
Oil on canvas, 8'2¼" x 11'11¾".
Private collection, Vaduz

LIKE TANGUY, Delvaux was influenced by de Chirico, and by the Surrealists, though never formally an adherent of their movement. He creates a world in which illogically juxtaposed dramatis personae move like sleepwalkers through inexplicable situations that seem to occasion them no surprise. At one time or another, almost everyone has dreamed of finding himself in public with no clothes on, but Delvaux's figures accept this predicament without embarrassment. All his characters, in fact, whether clothed or naked, are generally too self-engrossed to be aware of anyone else.

Delvaux derived the man in the frock coat at the left of the *Phases of the Moon* from an engraving by Edouard Riou illustrating a late-nineteenth-century edition of Jules Verne's *Journey to the Center of the Earth.* He represents the central character of that tale, the narrator's uncle, a German professor of "philosophy, chemistry, geology, mineralogy, and many other ologies." Delvaux has said that, as a child, he was so fascinated by this illustration that he made a copy of it to hang in his study. Years later, he recalled the figure and decided to incorporate it into a painting, selecting the subject of the moon's phases as appropriate to the scholar's scientific vocation. To counteract the figure's austerity, he placed him in an alien, disquieting setting peopled with nudes. The landscape background with its conical mountains may refer indirectly to Verne's novel, which was inspired by accounts of a scientist's descent into the flaming crater of Stromboli, though in the book the locale was moved to Iceland. The lighting of the scene is ambiguous. Is it day or night? Within a star-filled sky, the right side of the moon shines brightly; but lit from some unseen source at the left, all objects cast shadows that fall to the right.

Gazing with myopic intensity at the object in his hands, the learned man conforms to Verne's description of a savant who "was once known to classify six hundred different geological specimens by their weight, hardness, fusibility, sound, taste, and smell . . . My uncle was fifty years old; tall, thin, and wiry. Large spectacles hid, to a certain extent, his vast, round, and goggle eyes, while his nose was irreverently compared to a thin file." This figure copied from Riou's engraving, who makes his first appearance in Delvaux's art in the *Phases of the Moon,* has continued to haunt the artist's fantasies for more than twenty years, recurring in a number of other pictures.

Helen M. Franc

"I BELIEVE there is little to gain by exchanging opinions with other artists concerning either the ideology of art or technical methods. Very much alone in my work, I am almost jealous of it. Geography has no bearing on it, nor have the interests of the [artistic] community in which I work." Thus wrote Yves Tanguy in reply to a questionnaire on "The Creative Process" published in the magazine Art Digest in 1954.

Faced with such a carefully worded caveat, one hesitates to discuss his work at all. Nor do the paintings themselves invite description or analysis. Self-created, totally autonomous, they exist in a world where time, space, and light are functions of natural laws other than ours. Tanguy's landscapes, if they are landscapes, are not so much inhospitable as alien: neither vegetable nor mineral but an amalgam of both, absorbed in their own being, facing in another direction. "From the ends of the earth to the twilight of today/Nothing can withstand my desolate images," wrote Tanguy's friend Paul Eluard in a poem entitled "Yves Tanguy."

The swollen volumes and more fibrous, corruptible substances in some of the forties' paintings are in turn questioned, dissected, and parceled out in the work Tanguy did in the last five years of his life, culminating in his final masterpiece, The Museum of Modern Art's *Multiplication of Arcs*, which James Thrall Soby has called "a sort of boneyard of the world." Sometimes, in a work such as *Fear*, his aim seems analytical, as though he sought to break down large forms into their irregularly shaped components. These irreducible elements can be pebble-shaped, notched, pierced; occasionally they are long and painfully attenuated thorns. At other times, it looks as though the particles had drawn together to form a compact mass like a puzzle sphere.

John Ashbery

TANGUY: *Fear*. 1949.
Oil on canvas, 60 x 40".
Whitney Museum
of American Art, New York

RENE MAGRITTE invented a vocabulary of images which he has used and reused, transposed, changed the import of each image by changing their juxtaposition—much as one does with single words, meaning one thing in one sentence, acquiring a new significance when the verb is altered. He paints the "bewildering object" and the "accidental encounter." The method itself consists in isolating the object by breaking off its ties with the rest of the world in a more or less brutal or in a more or less insidious manner. We may cut off a hand and place it on the table, or we may paint the image of a cut-off hand on the wall. We may isolate by using a frame or by using a knife, but even more by a deformation, or a modification, in the substance of an object—a woman without a head, a hand of glass. Or by a change of scale—a lipstick the height of a forest. Or by a change of scenery—the Louis-Philippe table on a field of ice, a statue in a ditch.

Paul Nougé

I PAINTED pictures in which objects were represented with the appearance they have in reality, in a style objective enough to ensure that their upsetting effect—which they would reveal themselves capable of provoking owing to certain means utilitzed— would be experienced in the real world whence the objects had been borrowed. This by a perfectly natural transposition.

In my pictures I showed objects situated where we never find them. They represented the realization of the real if unconscious desire existing in most people.

The creation of new objects, the transformation of known objects, the change of matter for certain other objects, the association of words with images, the putting to work of ideas suggested by friends, the utilization of certain scenes from half-waking or dream states—all were means employed with a view to establishing contact between consciousness and the external world. The titles of the pictures were chosen in such a way as to inspire a justifiable mistrust of any tendency the spectator might have to overready self-assurance.

René Magritte

MAGRITTE:
Personal Values. 1952.
Oil on canvas, 31⅝ x 39½".
Collection Harry Torczyner,
New York

INFLUENCED by Klee and Ernst, Brauner had already experimented with visionary and "surrational" poetic imagery before settling in France in 1930. In Paris in 1932, he became a formal adherent of the Surrealist group, exhibiting paintings of a dream world developed in a hazy, illusionistic, "psychological" space, which also characterized the Surrealist paintings of Oscar Dominguez and, later, Matta. He himself has described these earlier works as paintings of an "unknown world . . . peopled with somnambulists, incubi, succubi . . . phantoms, specters, sorcerers, seers, mediums, and a whole fantastic population . . . insinuating, obsessing by its nebulous infusion; . . . the communication vessel of fire and water, being misty, vaporous, rainy, ectoplasmic, protoplasmic . . ." Whether in his early oneiric paintings or in his later pictographic works—such as *Prelude to a Civilization*—which can no longer be described as Surrealist, Brauner's primary concern and unifying theme is metamorphosis, including the containing, the generating of one form by another.

Breaking with the Surrealists in 1948, Brauner experienced a period of introspection. The anthropomorphic images of his paintings suggest that he took refuge in an inner world of psychodrama until, around 1951, he emerged into a more objective, externalized world in which reinvented symbols borrowed from archaic and primitive civilizations have replaced earlier dream images.

The pictographs which constitute *Prelude to a Civilization* recall the wall paintings of ancient Egypt: the luminous color, the delicate incision of small motifs into the ground, the decoratively flattened side views are, in this regard, quite specific. Brauner, however, refers to a private civilization in which the Paleolithic, African, and Persian are collectively recalled, while at the same time there may suddenly appear a profile of Picasso's, a motif of Klee's, or an inscription of de Chirico's.

Brauner's images are fragile yet, in their references, eternal. The pregnant, anthropomorphic images of *Prelude to a Civilization* refer to the theme of metempsychosis, or rebirth through an animal body; the founding of civilization through the intervention or medium of a benevolent animal is a myth which recurs from Islam to Rome.

Brauner's personal myth, here inscribed in wax on a blackened ground, takes on the physical presence of an ancient wall—gone are the vaporous mists and illusionistic spaces of earlier paintings. But Brauner's symbols are enigmatic; the narrative of the Egyptian walls and the Surrealist psychodrama are sacrificed for transcendent form. His is a modern vision of the timeless object.

Bernice Rose

THIS REMARKABLE picture recapitulates Dali's interests of the last twenty-five years. He has described it as "a quasi-gray picture: which, seen close up, is abstract; seen from two meters, is Raphael's *Sistine Madonna*; and, seen from fifteen meters, is the ear of an angel measuring a meter and a half; a picture which is painted with anti-matter, therefore with pure energy."

This homage to Raphael underscores Dali's allegiance to the academic tradition in painting. Vermeer, Velázquez, Raphael—"the most antiacademic, the most tenderly alive, and the most futuristic of the aesthetic archetypes of all times"—these are the orthodox heroes of the unorthodox Dali, whose avowed ambition has been to integrate the experiments of modern art with the great classical tradition.

DALI: *Madonna*. 1958.
Oil on canvas, 88⅞ x 75¼".
Collection Mr. and Mrs.
Henry J. Heinz II, London

In the fifties Dali became fascinated with nuclear physics, especially the concept of "antimatter." Particles of matter disappear on contact with particles of antimatter, releasing tremendous energy. The *Madonna* offers a kind of visual play on the anti-matter concept as the image "dissolves" and "reorganizes" itself, the product of Dali's "creative energy." The myriad dots that both integrate and explode the image recall a gigantic halftone reproduction, an instrument essential to our mass-media culture.

Upon this constantly shifting "atomic" screen Dali perversely superimposes impeccably painted *trompe l'oeil* elements: a piece of paper and, on a string, a cherry— "the fruit of Paradise" and a symbol of heaven. The "ultra-retrograde" super-realist technique again honors academicians such as Ernest Meissonier, while adding yet another layer to the illusion of art.

Dali's image evokes the whimsy of alchemistic transmutations and the Rabelaisian fantasy of Pantagruel's birth through the ear. It also plays mischievously on the Catholic doctrine of the virgin birth of Jesus, thought by some in medieval times to have similarly occurred by the way of the ear.

Besides, Dali loves angels. They are, after all, the most "antimaterial" of beings. Whether small enough, as in medieval legend, to land in hosts on the head of a pin or large enough to accommodate a Madonna and Child in an ear, they are indispensable to Dali's cosmogony, the magical stage where science and fantasy meet. "It is," he says, "with pi-mesons and the most gelatinous and indeterminate neutrinos that I want to paint the beauty of angels and of reality."

Susana Leval

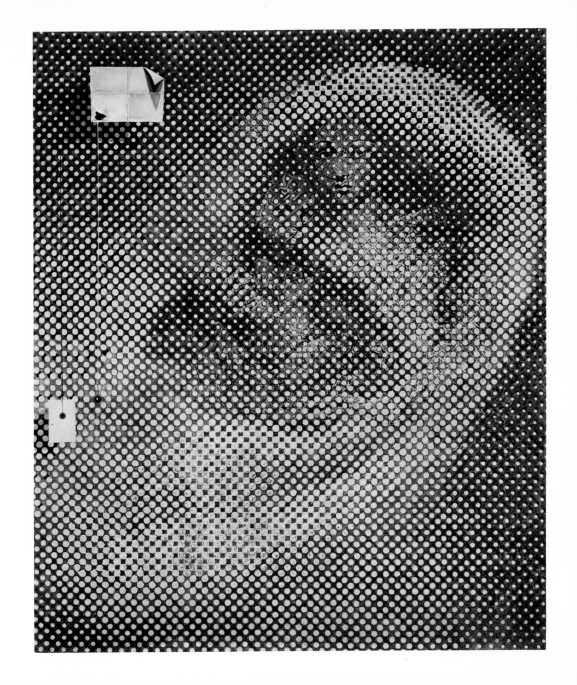

TEN PORTRAITS

THIS IS A directly painted portrait of a little girl dressed in an elegant tucked linen shirt and an overdress of ivory white stuff, like flannel, with an embroidered yoke and ivory buttons. The child, Lucie Bérard, was the daughter of a rich banker and former embassy secretary, Paul Bérard, who was one of the artist's major patrons. Here she stands at attention, in her best clothes, so that the painter could work from her.

Renoir applied scumbles of yellows and siennas over the white lead priming, then painted the background with thin and very free and uneven scumbles. In depicting the child, however, he applied a solid paint film and, in the costume areas, a considerable amount of delicate impasto. Renoir has drawn Lucie's hands with great care and clearly shows her smooth and soft flesh. Her head is rendered to appear solid and again the smooth skin is delicately painted, as is also her brilliant golden hair. She obviously had big blue eyes, and the painter very reasonably has made these the focal point of the picture. Surprisingly, Lucie is shown with her glance directed not at the spectator but slightly away from him.

As a work of art the painting not only evokes childhood in general, as well as a particular little girl, but it also is a brilliant piece of abstract design in the simplest of terms. There is no sense of space, only of light and color. And the sole indication of air is given by the slightly softened focus on Lucie's hands. The total impression is slightly uncompromising and a bit austere. This is perhaps the result of Renoir's own attitudes toward the progress of his work.

John Maxon

RENOIR: *Child in White.* 1883.
Oil on canvas, 24¼ x 19¾".
The Art Institute of Chicago.
Mr. and Mrs. Martin A. Ryerson
Collection

IF RENOIR commented joyously on life, then Toulouse-Lautrec was his opposite, for his comments were usually acid. Crippled and stunted at an early age by a fall from a horse, Toulouse-Lautrec, an aristocrat by birth, chose to live in the dissipation and squalor of Montmartre's low life. His subject matter was drawn from the night life of Paris: M. Boileau was a semigenteel bouncer for a Parisian scandal sheet, and his blue jowls, broad torso, and self-satisfied air seem most appropriate to his position. Toulouse-Lautrec delights in such tidbits as the stiff-necked, square-headed man to the right, or the incongruous combination of stovepipe hat and fur-collared coat of his tablemate. The deliberately tilted perspective of the tabletop is necessary as a foil for the expansive M. Boileau. The vibrating, artificial illumination of the café is a unifying factor, as is the hasty but incisive brushwork. The milky green of the liquid in the tumbler—undoubtedly absinthe—is a sinister accent as essential to this picture as the pink purse is to a portrait by Frans Hals. But the color, intensifying the mood of the picture, seems a fitting projection of the deformed artist's satiric interests, which were fittingly expressed with a linear mastery not unlike that of Degas.

Sherman Lee

DELIBERATELY, Toulouse-Lautrec detached himself from his own class to analyze a demimonde sometimes colorful and often sordid. All of his work was a form of portraiture. His observation was penetrating, acute in both a psychological and a social sense. Only for artistic reasons did he edit his analysis. Although his descriptions occasionally approach caricature, he was never a humorist. "I do not detail you. I totalize you," he once told Yvette Guilbert.

Very little is remembered about the sitter, not even his first name. But Toulouse-Lautrec must have studied him closely, and that he was a friend is known by the artist's dedication at the top left of the painting. The portrait was painted in the same year that Toulouse-Lautrec held his first exhibition, with Charles Maurin, at the Galerie Goupil on the Boulevard Montmartre. It was also included in the Salon des Indépendants of that year.

W.S.L.

TOULOUSE-LAUTREC:
M. Boileau in a Café. 1893.
Gouache on cardboard, 31½ x 25⅝".
The Cleveland Museum of Art.
Hinman B. Hurlbut Collection.
See color plate, page 17

THE *Artist with the Idol* perfectly recaptures Gauguin's powerful physique and enigmatic personality, described by a contemporary writer and friend, Charles Morice, in the winter of 1890: "A broad face, massive and bony, a narrow forehead, a nose neither curved nor arched, but as if broken, a thin-lipped mouth without any inflection, heavy eyelids lifting sluggishly over slightly protuberant eyeballs . . . There was little charm about this stranger; yet he attracted one by his very personal expression, a mixture of haughty nobility and of a simplicity that bordered on triviality."

In dress and physical appearance this self-portrait shows certain affinities to another portrait of Gauguin by Eugène Carrière, executed just before the former's departure to Tahiti in April of 1891. Interestingly, the pose is reminiscent of a photograph of 1888, in which Gauguin is shown relaxing in an armchair, his hand to his chin, wearing the same embroidered Breton peasant shirt as in the Carrière portrait.

Nevertheless, Gauguin probably executed *The Artist with the Idol* in Paris in the fall of 1893, after his first Tahitian sojourn. He is beardless and in Parisian attire. Furthermore, the figure in the right background, the Maori idol Hina, Moon goddess of night and love, provides a clue to the date. It is almost certainly an image of one of the two sculptures that Gauguin executed in Tahiti and brought back with him to Paris to be shown at the Durand-Ruel exhibition in November of 1893.

Gauguin often placed curious images in the backgrounds of his self-portraits. These acted as foils to the central image, widening its meaning with veiled allusions and ambiguous associations. In some self-portraits, these secondary images are overtly religious, identifying Gauguin with the martyred Christ and converting him to a symbol of all artists, outcasts of society, who suffer and sacrifice for their artistic ideals. In others, the association is with another more natural and carnal side of the artist's nature. It was this sensual side which Gauguin dreamed of liberating in Tahiti, far from the restraints of civilized life in Paris. Thus, the idol in this self-portrait at once evokes Gauguin's paradisiacal vision of a remote, mysterious culture, still unspoiled by civilization, and his ambiguous image of himself as a sensitive soul, akin to that alien people, yet ultimately isolated from it.

Susana Leval

GAUGUIN: *The Artist with the Idol. c. 1893.*

Oil on canvas, 17¼ x 12⅞".
Marion Koogler McNay
Art Institute, San Antonio.
Bequest of Marion Koogler McNay

ALTHOUGH SHY and reserved by nature—a listener rather than a talker—Vuillard was far from being misanthropic and deeply enjoyed social life in his mild way. He depended a great deal on his friends who, as one of them wrote, "opened and closed his horizons." As a young man his closest intimates had been fellow painters, grouped together as the "Nabis" (the Hebrew word for prophet), including, notably, Bonnard, Maurice Denis, K.-X. Roussel, and the theatrical impresario Lugné-Poë. From there he branched out into the literary and artistic circle dominated by the Natanson family, publishers of the famous magazine *La Revue Blanche* which championed many of the new aesthetic movements in the air around the turn of the century, particularly those embodying the principles and practice of Symbolism.

After 1900 Vuillard ventured still further in Paris social life, entering the rich and cultivated world of the French upper bourgeoisie, a world in which Mme Arthur Fontaine, portrayed here, was a leading figure. The wife of an important industrialist, and sister-in-law of the composer Ernest Chausson, she held, in her apartment near the Invalides, musical gatherings frequented by Debussy, Gide, Valéry, Claudel, and others. A discriminating, energizing hostess, she was one of the Egerias who, throughout his life, pushed Vuillard forward when diffidence might have held him back. In fact, one cannot understand his essentially genial art without reference to the kind of society he cultivated.

This radiant portrait, flickering with luscious, sun-drenched, ever so subtly harmonized color, takes us some distance from the narrow, doctrinaire Nabi aesthetic of Vuillard's youth. It harks back to Impressionism, in that form shimmers, quasi-dissolved in light and atmosphere, and windows look out onto the sky. Like many Vuillard portraits of this period, around 1900, it can hardly be described as a striking likeness, nor was it intended as such. Mme Fontaine stands far away from the artist, actually turning her back on him. She is a memorable figure, dressed in a pink, light, almost transparent robe, representing not so much herself as her refined ambience, opulent yet distinguished. Nonetheless the result is highly personal, one of the most delightful tributes that an artist could pay to a life of leisure and ease. "The figures are hardly necessary," wrote a critic about Vuillard's work. "We divine their presence from the surroundings. No artist has ever so suggested the soul of an interior—the sense of habitation."

Stuart Preston

VUILLARD: *Mme Arthur Fontaine.* c. 1900.
Oil on cardboard, 24⅞ x 22½".
Private collection, New York

THIS ASTONISHING self-portrait, done at the very end of Bonnard's life, resembles not at all the amiably inquisitive looks he had taken at himself in earlier years. If the face is the window of the human body, and more than suffices as a depiction of personality, this painting contains a stricken image, an excruciating image of self, and the rare appearance of abnormal expressive power hardly found elsewhere in his urbane, detached art. There is no self-pity in this characterization, but it does show signs of suffering.

The portrait's date furnishes an essential clue to the presence of this latter quality. Like all sensitive Frenchmen, Bonnard had suffered deeply under the German Occupation. However, a far more catastrophic grief had been the recent death of his wife. Ever since the 1890s, she had been his closest and only real intimate. They were childless. Now, here, he is alone and old and despairing. No wonder this self-portrait is a haunting one.

There may yet be another explanation for the slight air of unreality here, for the tremulous paint handling, and for the ambiguous vagueness of the background, a sort of flickering mosaic of emotional color. All his life Bonnard had been myopic. No portrait or photograph shows him without his spectacles. But now he doffs them and gazes at himself mercilessly.

The self-portrait is a fascinating genre, providing, as Max J. Friedlander wrote, "the psychologist with an opportunity for stimulating speculation. Externally it may be recognized through the glance directed decisively at the spectator—since the painter looked at himself in a mirror—and the attention, seemingly addressed to us, was devoted to his own appearance. This entails a self-revelation, an emergence from the picture to a degree which usually is not characteristic of portraits. Man does not take up a neutral or objective attitude toward his own appearance; his participation is colored more by his 'will' than by his 'idea.' Self-portraits do not confirm the view that we know ourselves better than others. They are not in a particularly high degree 'good likenesses.' "

Stuart Preston

BONNARD: *Self-Portrait.* 1945.
Oil on canvas, 22 x 18".
Collection Mr. and Mrs.
Donald S. Stralem, New York

THOSE WHO look for consistency in an artist's work and find in it a logical progression, changing over the years but always stylistically personal and recognizable, have always been puzzled, and even dismayed, by the apparently contradictory course taken by André Derain's art. That he was a major twentieth-century French artist is undeniable. But how does one reconcile his dazzling early Fauve landscapes and his solider, Cézanne-Cubist pictures done on the eve of World War I with the delightful Corot-like landscapes and Chardinesque still lifes of later years? The truth is that Derain's art was at the mercy of a capricious, restless intelligence, always in search of some original alliance between "modern" art and the old masters.

That he wholly succeeded in this ambition was doubted even by himself. Illuminatingly enough, he once declared that "everyone ought to find the wine that suits him; a wine exists for every palate." "Have you found yours?" he was asked. "No," he replied.

One of his most impressive paintings is the severe and majestic portrait of the Basque artist Francesco de Iturrino (1864–1924). Sober and restrained in tone, totally rejecting his earlier Fauve use of color for expressive purposes, it illustrates that by 1914 (the date of this portrait) Derain, influenced by Cézanne and Cubism, had undertaken an austere investigation of pictorial structure and human character. Nor can one miss his increasing interest in the old masters. The gaunt head may be geometrically analyzed, but the whole noble presentation of the subject recalls Tintoretto and, more closely, El Greco in the elongation of form, particularly in the strong hands and in the dramatic contrasts of light and dark.

Despite these mixed stylistic concerns, Derain does not fail to achieve a good and sympathetic likeness. Behind the motif—that is, the sitter—Derain makes us aware that he is portraying truthfully a human being for whom he cares. Daring and discipline were, as Guillaume Apollinaire observed, two of Derain's chief characteristics. Or, as the artist once himself remarked to a critic: "I am not attached to any principle—except that of liberty. But my idea of liberty is that it must be related to tradition." Nowhere in the complex course of his art is this conviction better embodied than in the portrait of Iturrino.

Stuart Preston

DERAIN: *Francesco de Iturríno.* 1914.

Oil on canvas, 36¼ x 25⅝".
Musée National d'Art Moderne, Paris.
Gift of Mme Geneviève Gallibert

MODIGLIANI'S sitter is a friend—Manuello Humbert, a painter from Barcelona who was president of a group of young Spanish artists in Paris. There is another Modigliani portrait of Humbert, perhaps slightly earlier, in the Los Angeles County Museum.

The Melbourne work is a three-quarter view. Humbert is a very composed sitter; he is conscious of the painter, very straight and dignified in his pose, a conscientious sitter with an almost finical composure. His hands are precisely placed on his knees, his mouth is small and pursed, his slightly protruding ears are carefully outlined. In the upright formal pose his tie has slipped a little and is slightly informal. (Sometimes in Modigliani's portraits the tie or the neckpiece has a sensuous vitality within the austere design.) The care of inscription that marks out the features of this face is typical of the abstract and patterning way in which Modigliani works on his portraits. Inspired by the precise treatment of features in primitive art and the contemporary experiments of the School of Paris, Modigliani formed a personal art in which traditional subjects were given a new simplicity of form. In the Humbert portrait he uses his line to separate and call attention to the features of his sitter: he accentuates the arcs of the eyebrows and makes the eyes clear pointed ovals with numbered lashes. The manneristic outline lengthens the face, twists the nose out of symmetry, and points the chin around the small mouth. The precision of the features is transferred to the personality of the sitter.

The somber quality of the paint increases the quiet appreciation which we feel to be the relation between painter and sitter. The chocolate-colored background with its suggestion of squares and faint abstract patterning almost absorbs the sitter's suit of the same color; the clothes disappear to leave the warm orange oval of the face and the hands far below. The composure of the hands, so simply painted and precisely placed, enhances the trusting dignity of Humbert. As in all Modigliani portraits, there is a feeling of wistfulness and melancholy, of unresisting figures trapped by lines that become an enclosure of sadness.

Ursula Hoff and Margaret Plant

MODIGLIANI: *Portrait of a Man.*
1917.
Oil on canvas, 39½ x 25⅝".
National Gallery of Victoria,
Melbourne. Felton Bequest

WITH ONE exception Miró's early paintings had been landscapes and still lifes. During the winter of 1917-18, however, he turned to portraying the human figure.

In Barcelona, Miró painted six portraits of men, perhaps beginning with this examination of himself. He was not yet twenty-five, he had not yet visited Paris. That he was acquainted with examples of Fauve and Cubist painting, however, is known and demonstrated here. Another portrait in the series suggests that he may have also studied Delaunay. A review of the sequence of these six portraits illustrates the rapid evolution of Miró's first mature style.

In the picture, there is little space behind or in front of the figure. The contour of the face combines a variety of strident colors which are not repeated elsewhere. For some reason, and true of all six portraits, Miró seems to have had most difficulty in painting the lips which, curiously, are thickened as well as pursed. The portrait has a slightly awkward, bumpkin aspect.

The flat background is green. A thick, almost continuous band of yellow silhouettes the figure. Brushstrokes of the same color highlight details of the face, dot the bow tie, and, at the right, overpaint the brown and black coat. Two years later, in 1919, Miró painted a second self-portrait which he brought to Paris and sold to his fellow countryman Picasso. This portrait is a nearer likeness, without the jowly cheeks. How different, also, is Balthus' portrait of Miró completed in 1938 (page 225).

Examples of Miró's Surrealist paintings are reproduced on pages 185 and 187.

W.S.L.

MIRO: *Self-Portrait.* 1917.
Oil on canvas, 24 x 19⅝".
The Bragaline Collection,
New York

220

IN BERLIN and in Cologne, immediately after the armistice of World War I, artists and writers responded to the shrill call of Dada, a revolutionary and iconoclastic attitude which in life, art, and literature mocked the status quo. In Berlin, Dada was particularly characterized by a bitter contempt for the folly of the war and by despair at the resulting economic and moral debacle. George Grosz, throughout his life a moralist, was a leader of Berlin Dada.

Subsequently, during the Weimar Republic, George Grosz won rapid and notorious fame for the savage satire of his drawings in black and white. Unfortunately, his brilliance as a draftsman, first as a Dadaist and then as a cartoonist, has obscured his considerable achievement as a painter. "Most people," he realized, "have never appreciated the artistic element in my work; they have been aware only of the subject matter and its political implications." As a painter Grosz can be ranked, if not with Daumier, certainly with Hogarth.

By 1925, when Grosz returned to painting in oil, artistic attitudes in Germany were in transition and, often, opposition. The fever of Expressionism and the anarchy of Dada had subsided. Indeed by 1922, Dada as an historical movement was dead. There were also negative responses to abstraction as well as to the philosophy and disciplines of the Bauhaus School. One of the strongest of these inevitable reactions was a new attention to realism. Grosz's painting of his friend, the poet Max Herrmann-Neisse, illustrates the "new objectivity" as it was called in Germany at the time. The portrait also captures a mood of sadness, resignation, even pessimism.

A second portrait by Grosz of Herrmann-Niesse, also painted in 1927, was purchased by the Museum at Mannheim. Later, it was confiscated by the Nazis. For them it was a perfect example of "degenerate art"! The subject was not only a Jew but a hunchback.

W.S.L.

GROSZ: *Max Herrmann-Neisse.*
1927.
Oil on canvas, 23⅜ x 29⅛".
The Museum of Modern Art, New York

IN THIS double portrait, Balthus stubbornly adheres to the realist tradition and, taking the nineteenth-century artist Courbet as his model, painstakingly seeks to render an exact physical likeness of his sitters. For this painting, Miró and his daughter posed nearly every day for three months. In order to make them stay still, Balthus rigged up wooden blocks to hold their feet in place—undoubtedly an ordeal for a lively little girl, and probably for her father, too, judging by his rather set expression.

The tender relationship between father and daughter, as well as the resemblance between them, nevertheless comes through. It is conveyed principally by the position of the hands—Miró's showing the gentlest restraint, Dolores' a confiding affection. The horizontal line marking the juncture of floor and wall divides the composition precisely midway. The sober, unornamented background, without a single detail to detract attention from the figures, serves as foil to the vertical stripes and red piping of the child's dress.

Helen M. Franc

BALTHUS: *Joan Miró and His Daughter Dolores.* 1937-38.
Oil on canvas, 51¼ x 35".
The Museum of Modern Art, New York.
Abby Aldrich Rockefeller Fund

THE SCHOOL of PARIS: TEN PAINTERS

THIS LYRICAL cityscape, painted toward 1900, acknowledges in a personal way Bonnard's debt to Impressionism, while also introducing elements foreign to the Impressionist aesthetic. The big city was a dominating element in late-nineteenth-century French life, and figured largely in its art. One has only to think of the glittering pageant of Paris boulevards as portrayed by Monet and Pissarro, not to mention an artist like Jean Béraud, whose work has come so strongly into favor in recent years.

On the other hand, looked at more closely, *Boulevard de Clichy* might well be considered anti-Impressionist in a number of ways. The figures exert greater importance than the background. Light, weather, and time of day are ambiguous, while the sky, that Impressionist forte, has been totally suppressed. Thus, although the painting purports to depict an actual scene, it is slightly artificial in concept and there is a minimum of open-air feeling.

What it does remind us of is a stage set complete with figures: the low iron fence bordering the grass plot in the foreground stands for the forward edge of the proscenium on which the cast of characters parades. This distinct feeling of artificiality and the low-keyed dramatic interpretation of the figures owe much to Nabi interest in the theater and in decorative effects. Unlike the Impressionists, Bonnard and his fellow-Nabis had worked as stage designers, made posters, and executed fanciful murals for private houses, in all of which endeavors liberties had been taken with natural appearances. Nonetheless, *Boulevard de Clichy* is generically an Impressionist picture in which everyday life is depicted with refined and witty observation. He shows wonderful facility in capturing the bustling, yet empty, character of a street scene. Color is subdued and discreet here, Bonnard favoring at this moment close grayish harmonies with few strong accents. It was only later in his painting career that he developed the rich, almost visionary harmonies that beat the Impressionists on their own ground.

Stuart Preston

BONNARD: *Boulevard de Clichy*. c. 1900.
Oil on canvas, 25¾" x 36¼".
Private collection, New York

AESTHETIC revolutions are apt to be launched with daring manifestos. That of the Nabi movement, Vuillard's first powerful impetus, was sounded off by the painter Maurice Denis at the age of nineteen! "Remember," he wrote in his *Définition du Néo-Traditionnisme*, published in 1890, "that before it is a war-horse, a naked woman, or a trumpery anecdote, a painting is essentially a flat surface covered with colors assembled in a certain order."

Vuillard had little interest in abstract principles per se. Although he generally agreed with this definition, he qualified it in practice with what Denis later identified as his—Vuillard's—special qualities, lucidity and vigilance.

Painted in 1891, *Girls Walking* is an example of his Nabi style at its purest. Here we observe a bold simplification of forms, contrasting areas of flat color used for a decorative effect with little representational function, and a strong rhythmical surface design derived in part from Japanese prints. Anecdotal interest is eschewed, the banality of the subject matter suggesting little beyond itself. It must have appeared stark and crude in 1891, when pictures telling a story, preferably a touching one, were all the rage.

However, in the light of subsequent knowledge of Vuillard's pictorial sympathies, we can just detect here a foreshadowing of the kind of Intimism that he was to make so triumphantly his own. Whereas this painting may fully demonstrate Nabi theory, it conveys, too, hints of the mysterious poetic meaning in everyday life—the Symbolist "air of things," nonspecific in feeling, not overtly sentimental but emanating sympathies with things known and cherished.

An aura of secrecy envelops a proto-Intimist painting such as this one. As André Gide wrote about them: "M. Vuillard speaks almost in a whisper—as is only right when confidences are being exchanged—and we have to bend over toward him to hear what he says." We grasp the color pattern before we identify the elusive, apparently meaningless subject matter whose poetic significance simply exists on its own. Vuillard was well aware of the intensely private character of these little pictures. Late in life, when exhibiting them publicly for the first time, he exclaimed anxiously: "It's dreadful, revealing all these secrets."

Stuart Preston

VUILLARD: *Girls Walking.* 1891.
Oil on canvas, 32 x 25⅝".
Private collection, New York

VUILLARD'S high-spirited, irresistibly droll youthful self-portrait is unusual in his work. For one thing, he depicts himself as a dandy—a role alien to his character—all dressed up in a frock coat, carrying a fancy walking stick, and perching on his already balding head a straw "boater," the height of male fashion in the early 1890s, the period of this painting. Furthermore he reveals in this portrait the sense of humor that his solemn manner usually concealed.

Vuillard and his Nabi friends, principally Bonnard, Maurice Denis, and K.-X. Roussel, were serious enough in their youthful defiance of what they considered to be the arterio-sclerosis of academicism and the all too fluent naturalism of the Impressionists. They would meet in the evenings to plot the sensational new simplifications they planned to incorporate in their art, hoping to set off a bomb under the Establishment. And, being young, they would indulge in childish mystifications such as odd costumes, passwords, and private nicknames. Because of his short, military-style beard (evident here), Vuillard was known as the "Zouave." But however much he subscribed to the Nabis' radical ideas of the reformation of art, he had far less interest in their endless theorizing. At one meeting he referred irritably to Gauguin, the Nabi idol, as a "pedant." Developing his own sensibility and probing his own emotions were more important to him than redefining complex intellectual aims.

Usually silent but attentive during such discussions, Vuillard could be witty in a quiet manner, as in this compact little painting, which anticipates the Fauves by about fifteen years. In this portrait he carries Nabi theories to almost absurd lengths, depicting himself in terms of a flat pattern of pure expressive color, his physical appearance being at one with the wallpaper, and totally eliminating depth, modeling, and shadow. "So much for painting strictly by formula" would seem to be the message sent out by this vital little glimpse of himself. It pokes gentle fun at the aesthetic fanaticism of some of his companions. Theory could point the way to self-realization, but obeying one's instincts was, in the long run, the more rewarding course. He followed the latter and he arrived.

Vuillard was, briefly, close to Toulouse-Lautrec. At almost the same time that he painted this self-portrait, Vuillard also painted his artist friend. Toulouse-Lautrec kept the portrait, and it is now in the Museum at Albi. Both paintings are similar in size, composition, and colors.

Stuart Preston

VUILLARD: *Self-Portrait.* 1892.
Oil on canvas, 14⅜ x 11⅛".
Collection Mr. and Mrs. Ralph F. Colin, New York

ONE COULD make a fascinating anthology of uncharacteristic work by major artists, work usually done in youth when, casting about in search of a truly personal style, they would experiment with modes that appeared to be most vital at the moment. Such aesthetic adventuring was most often of brief duration, as styles temporarily adhered to soon were found wanting, or were alien to the artist's basic aesthetic character.

No such anthology should omit Dufy's short flirtation (for that it was and never a submission) with Cubism (1908–10). A Cubist Dufy! one will exclaim. What a contradiction in terms. Could his high-spirited hedonism ever have been tamed, even slightly, by the solemn, intellectual objectivity of the Cubists, whose analytical style excluded all the sensuous and witty elements that make his art so irresistibly appealing? Yet such was the case, and here is one of the rare examples of geometrical simplification in his sparkling output.

Beginning as a talented follower of the Impressionists, Dufy next became one of the most brilliant Fauves, having succumbed to Matisse's *Luxe, Calme et Volupté* of 1905. "Studying that picture," he wrote, "I understood the essence of painting; Impressionistic realism lost all of its charm for me when contemplating that miracle of the imagination translated into design and color." But Fauvism was for him (and for most of the other Fauves) no more than an episode on the road to final self-identification. He wanted something to strengthen its simple expressiveness. For a time he found this structure in Cubism under the influence of Braque, also a former Fauve.

This harbor scene will hardly be defined by purists as a strictly Cubist picture. It sticks too much to purely visual facts, although they are somewhat geometrically simplified. "Constructed" it may be, and done in an unusually sober harmony of greens. Yet one can detect, in the liveliness of the boats, in the big spreading branches of the tree, and in the tumult of rising hills in the background, something of Dufy's essentially baroque style. He would not long persist in this ascetic divagation. Strength of draftsmanship would suffice for the constructive framework in his fully mature work.

Stuart Preston

DUFY: *Boats at Dock, Marseilles.* 1908.

Oil on canvas, 28¾ x 23⅝".
Musée National d'Art Moderne, Paris.
Bequest of the artist's wife

LIKE SEURAT, Modigliani died young. In the case of both painters one must ask how much further their development could have progressed. And in the case of Modigliani, as with van Gogh, the romance of the artist's life conspired to lend passion to his actual achievement. Like Picasso, Modigliani conceived the artist to be a superior being, and he lived and died by this belief.

Modigliani was a facile painter, intuitively lyric and elegant. The pictures by which he is known to the general public were painted during five brief years, 1915 to 1919. They constitute a production limited in time, subject, and style. He is not an artist who can easily sustain a large or comprehensive exhibition. His nudes, his greatest accomplishments, clearly reveal him as an Italian painter. Their attitudes suggest Titian. Their clarity of contour and lustrous form recall the sculptural paintings of Bronzino. The elongation, indeed deformation, of the body echoes Pontormo. Modigliani also employs the Mannerists' device of dark backgrounds to silhouette the figure. Indeed, in Modigliani's nudes the artistic individuality of the Mannerists finds its heritage. Such Italianate painting had not been produced in France since the School of Fontainebleau.

Modigliani began his series of great nudes in 1917. The format of several—about a dozen—offers the only horizontal images in Modigliani's entire *oeuvre*. The complete human figure is seldom rendered; hands, particularly fingers, always presented problems, and Modigliani never attempted to depict feet. Despite the sophistication of rendition, these models completely lack self-consciousness. They are splendidly voluptuous and often unabashed. The flesh tones vary and the colors, although monotonous, are warm and seductive. Here, the model is as aware of the painter as he is of her. The figure stretches across the canvas, and its cropped elbow and legs advance the spectator to the image. Such a nude invites dalliance, but there is nothing lascivious in the offering.

In December 1917, in Paris at Berthe Weill's gallery on the Rue Taitbout, Modigliani gathered together about thirty of his works. The exhibition was his first one-man show, and it included a few of the nudes which he had recently completed. Two of these, displayed in the window, were judged a public scandal; the gendarmerie of the préfecture closed the exhibition.

W.S.L.

MODIGLIANI: *Reclining Nude.* 1917.
Oil on canvas, 25½ x 39½".
Collection Richard S. Zeisler, New York

"IT WAS the war that brought me back to earth."

Léger's stint as an engineer in World War I had restored contact with the reality and solidity of life after the somewhat remote aestheticism of his Cubist phase. The experience had a crucial, irrevocable effect on his pictorial style: "Once I had bitten into this reality, the object was and remained essential to me."

Immediately after the war, Léger produced highly abstract studies inspired by mechanical forms; their reality parallels rather than duplicates that of machines. Then, slowly, human figures reappear in Léger's work: "After the dynamism of the mechanical phase, I felt a need for the static quality of the large forms. Earlier, I had broken up the human body. Now I began to put it together again." Yet the human figures reappear, "not as a sentimental element, but solely as a plastic element." Indeed, in the extraordinary figure compositions dating from 1920 onward, the human figures seem little more than "beautiful objects" made to conform to the rigid confines of their lucid, abstract environments.

People in a Garden is an example of Léger's private renaissance at the end of the "mechanical" period. An ordinary domestic interior scene has been transformed into a hieratic image of grandiose proportions. The figures, though treated as still-life objects, are elevated to a new level of dignity by the intense magnification and monumental scale. The volume and solidity of the figures are assimilated into the flatness of the severe, geometric surroundings through the echoing repetitions and connecting lines and forms.

In works of this period Léger shifts from the geometric analysis of Cézanne to the simple monumentality of the Douanier Rousseau. The factureless, austere finish Léger attributes to the latter's influence; the smooth gray shading, to training in photographic retouching. A restrained, elegant color balance also bespeaks the new classicism. Indeed, Léger had, in these monumental compositions, reached his avowed aim: "My purpose is to give certitude in art." He had rendered classical harmony and stability in a totally modern pictorial statement.

Susana Leval

LEGER: *People in a Garden.*
1922.
Oil on canvas, 25⅝ x 36¼".
Collection Mr. and Mrs. Allan D. Emil,
New York

IN 1922 Braque began a series of monumental figure paintings. These were the first he had undertaken since *The Musician* of 1917, and for them too he now found a wholly surprising, new pictorial technique. Stylistically, in fact, this series of figures is quite unlike anything else in the whole of Braque's work. The first two paintings were classical in inspiration and conceived as "Decorations." They represent Canephorae, young women who carried on their heads ceremonial baskets of fruit and flowers in the Panathenaic procession. As forerunners for Braque's conception of these women, one may cite the caryatids (fifth century B.C.) supporting the entablature of the Erechtheum on the Acropolis, or a so-called *Dancer* in bronze (circa 30 B.C.) from Herculaneum, or various decorative figures used architecturally in Italian Renaissance villas. There is also a basket-carrying maiden by Nicolas Poussin among the figures on the extreme right of *The Triumph of Flora* (circa 1628). Braque was surely aware of this past history, for its influence shows in his own *Canephorae*. Yet it is reasonable to guess that the idea for these two figures—which were quickly followed by others—was nurtured in Braque's mind by more contemporary sources. First, when Braque exhibited three paintings at the Salon d'Automne in October 1920, he saw there a commemorative exhibition of works by Renoir which included many large, fleshy nudes of his last years. Secondly, by 1920 a neoclassical reaction against revolution and fragmentation in the arts was taking hold in Paris. And thirdly, it is not unjustified to regard Braque's *Canephorae* as being to some extent his rejoinder to the series of monumental female figures—for example, *Three Women at a Spring* of 1921, directly inspired by classical originals—which dominate Picasso's work between 1919 and 1922.

Nevertheless, Braque created for the representation of the human figure an idiom which was wholly personal and keyed it to the rest of his painting. The forms which Braque gave to human bodies are ample, his modeling is broad and loose. And these two factors, aided by a delectable palette of brown, creamy yellow, and lime green, endow these figures with a tactile value which stops short of sensuality. These half-exposed female figures exist on a detached plane of semireality. They appear to be presented with the opulent fullness of a Rubens nude, yet they do not exist in the round. They seem to stand out in bold relief, yet they are soft, flattened, and inseparable from their mural background. On the other hand, they communicate a sense of movement, flux, and palpitation, which is absent from Braque's contemporary still lifes, because he makes great play with free linear rhythms, which he was subsequently to develop into a graphically decorative idiom.

Douglas Cooper

BRAQUE: *Canephorae*. 1922.
Oil on canvas, each 71¼ x 28¾".
Musée National d'Art Moderne, Paris.
The Baroness Napoléon Gourgaud
Bequest

FROM 1924 to 1926, Picasso produced a series of large and magnificently colored still-life compositions. All are more or less in the Cubist tradition, though often the shapes of objects are preserved without radical deformation or dissection. On the whole the series is objective and formal in spirit, untroubled by psychological or aesthetic experiment. In the *Studio* of 1925, Picasso returns to the right angle and straight line in the most compactly and intricately organized of the series. The fragments of sculpture—arms and head—reappear in a very different role twelve years later in the *Guernica*. In the background, the architecture which seems to imply a view through a window is actually part of the still life since it was painted from a toy theater belonging to Picasso's son. Here he translates it into Cubist terms not unlike those which he used five years previously for the settings of the ballet *Pulcinella*.

The *Studio* is extremely rich in color, in form, and even in texture. The great still-life series continues through the rest of 1925 and even after the *Three Dancers*, the painting of the same year in the Tate Gallery in London, so very similar in color but so radically different in spirit that it marks the beginning of a new period in Picasso's work.

Alfred H. Barr, Jr.

PICASSO: *Studio with Plaster Head.* 1925.
Oil on canvas, 38⅝ x 51⅝".
The Museum of Modern Art, New York

ALTHOUGH curved contours characterize many of his works of the late 1920s, Picasso passed to opposite and completely linear extremes in *The Studio*. This large and precisely calculated composition of rectangles and straight lines seems at first glance to be an abstract picture. It is not.

We see an artist at work, a theme frequent in Picasso's art. In a room stands the painter, palette and brush in either hand. At the right is his subject—a table, again dressed by a red tablecloth, on which rest a *compotier* with a single fruit and, on a base, a white plaster head. The eyes and mouth of the sculpture are placed vertically, as are those of the artist himself. The sharp, aggressive angles which outline the figure, cloth, bowl, and bust are stabilized by the strict rectangles of the mirror and picture frame on the wall and, at left and right, the larger easel and door. In addition, Picasso emphasizes the rectangular format of the picture by a black line and, parallel to it, a thin strip of frame painted white. The still life on the table is comparable to that in the earlier studio of 1925, page 243. Here, however, it is realized completely without modeling or detail and with a flatness of paint as well as of design.

Straight lines, dislocated dots of eyes, thumb hole, and table-leg tips recall drawings by Picasso in 1926 which were engraved as woodcuts and added to his illustrations to Balzac's *Le Chef-d'Oeuvre Inconnu* etched the following year. The spare and linear discipline of the delineation also relates the painting to a specific sculpture of the same period, notably Picasso's monument to his deceased and beloved friend, the poet Guillaume Apollinaire. The maquette for the monument was constructed in light iron rods.

W.S.L.

PICASSO: *The Studio*. 1927-28.
Oil on canvas, 59 x 91".
The Museum of Modern Art, New York
Gift of Walter P. Chrysler, Jr.

SOUTINE, Jules Pascin, Maurice Utrillo, and Modigliani—they have been grouped together as though violence of temper and proneness to trouble constituted a school of art. In France they are called *les peintres maudits*—painters under a curse. The lives of some Post-Impressionists, notably Gauguin and van Gogh, have put in the general mind and in the repertory of journalism about art a concept of melodramatic greatness. Here was another such generation.

Modigliani, even in the year of his death, drugged and debilitated, kept his extraordinary facility, and never departed from his same felicitous type of picture until the end. Pascin indulged his sensuality and wild, cynical humor until it turned to despair, then resolutely cut his life short; he did not linger over it to say what it meant. Utrillo's alcoholism and illness were a living death for many years.

Soutine was the least calamitous and least dissipated of the four, but perhaps the saddest. For as his art developed, it offered no distraction from his anxieties, animosities, and self-reproach—no escape. Not that he intended any effect of autobiography by means of his art. But from an early age he used his hardship, pessimism, and truculence to set a tragic tone for his painting, irrespective of its subject matter. Limiting the themes of his work to conventional categories—still life, landscape, portraiture, and picturesque figure painting—he would always charge his pictures with extreme implications of what he had in mind: violence of nature, universality of hunger, and a peculiar mingling of enthusiasms and antipathies.

Chartres Cathedral seems to have been intended as a piece of mysticism, glorifying and rejoicing, yet solemn. It is in jewel-colors, but not this time the famous intense shades suggestive of passion and sacrifice; instead, an extraordinary range of delicate tints, an opalescence—greenish blue and gray of seawater, and a bit of vivid rosiness like quartz. It seems a tribute of one art to the other, the contemporary easel painter gladly sacrificing some of his individualism to the great work of the collective medieval architects; its intricacies of structure, minutiae of carved stone and inset glass, all simply and fervently rendered.

How different Utrillo's view of the same facade painted, probably in his studio, twenty years before. Both paintings were first shown together in The Museum of Modern Art's tenth-anniversary exhibition *Art in Our Time* in 1939.

Monroe Wheeler

SOUTINE: *Chartres Cathedral.*
1933.
Oil on wood, 36⅜ x 19¾".
The Museum of Modern Art, New York.
Gift of Mrs. Lloyd Bruce Wescott

UTRILLO: *Chartres Cathedral.*
1913.
Oil on canvas, 36⅜" x 25¾".
Collection Mr. and Mrs.
Alex M. Lewyt, New York

IN THE *Guéridon* of 1935 (also titled *The Pedestal Table*), Braque has taken as a point of departure the sort of tabletop still life he was painting around 1930, but has used another type of brass-legged *guéridon*. This time, however, Braque has set out to enrich the general effect and expand the pictorial space with his most recent pictorial discoveries. Thus he has articulated the space behind the still life, as he had in the past, with two differently colored intersecting planes of blue and pale ocher running from bottom to top. But Braque has also expanded the tabletop to the right by a broad, curving white line surrounding its edge, and to the left by a pronounced arc which runs from the bunch of grapes to the flap of the tablecloth. Braque has then made great play between the voluminous, tactile fruit in the immediate right foreground, the stylized and insubstantial bunch of grapes, which acts as a formal link between the flaps of the cloth and the patterned wallpaper, and the massive but transparent glass in the background, which is again palpable. And as an ironical comment on the artificiality of the world conjured up by the painter, Braque has made the framed painting of fruit in a dish, hanging on the wall above the still life, wholly insubstantial by representing it with a web of lines drawn over the patterned wallpaper, so that even its situation in space is ambivalent. Thus, in this picture Braque combined the massive, the insubstantial, the palpable, the stylized, and the arbitrary in an image which is both convincing and decorative.

Douglas Cooper

BRAQUE: *The Pedestal Table.*
1935.
Oil on canvas, 70¼ x 28½".
The San Francisco Museum of Art.
Purchased through a gift of
W. W. Crocker

IN 1936 Braque—then aged fifty-four—embarked once again on a succession of masterly works. These are eminently personal in conception, inventive, marvelously organized, confident in execution, subtly if not always strongly colored, richly ornamented, and once again spatially involved. Certain characteristics recur throughout: a granular frescolike surface, a decorative pattern which is a stylization of either a bunch of grapes, a flower, or a bird, a paneled wooden dado, emphatic linear rhythms, zigzag, diamond, and serpentine motifs, and an overall surface animation. Yet, busy though they are, these are no longer flat, decorative compositions. On the contrary, objects once again have volume and are set in space. Braque claimed that by this time he had made the discovery "that ornament liberates color from form" and the workings of this dissociation are self-evident. In these pictures Braque created a richly orchestrated synthesis of free form, controlled color, and organized rhythm, which he embellished with arbitrarily disposed ornamental motifs and "rhymes." "So far as I am concerned," Braque said in an interview with Georges Charbonnier in 1950, "it is the rhyme which intervenes accidentally that gives life and spontaneity to a picture." Each of the pictorial elements functions in these pictures independently and simultaneously. But to contain so much activity Braque had to expand the pictorial space; he also introduced a more active play of light and shade.

In *Still Life with Mandolin* of 1936, Braque has bent the wall on the left so as to situate the console table in a shallow alcove, while the curves which are arbitrarily drawn across the background wall evoke a larger surface than the tabletop would have. These also have the effect of tilting the still life toward the spectator and making it more tangible.

Douglas Cooper

BRAQUE: *Still Life with Mandolin.* 1936.
Oil on canvas, 38¼ x 51¼".
Norton Gallery of Art,
West Palm Beach

A GENERATION before young American artists like James Rosenquist began to use Pop culture as a basis for their work, the French master Léger discovered that "bad taste is one of the valuable raw materials" of this country. As an artist in exile during the Occupation of France, Léger lived in the United States from 1940 to 1945 and traveled extensively across the continent. He was impressed by America's "vitality, its litter and its waste," its quest for novelty, its dynamism, and "the contrast between the mechanical and the natural." Especially, he pointed out: "Bad taste—strong colors —it is all here for the painter to organize and get the full use of its power. Girls in sweaters with brilliant-colored skin; girls in shorts dressed more like acrobats in a circus than one would ever come across on a Paris street. If I had only seen girls dressed in 'good taste' here I would never have painted my Cyclist series, of which *Big Julie* in The Museum of Modern Art was the culmination."

Needless to say, Léger transformed this raw material in accordance with his own predilections and distinctive style. The *Big Julie* combines his love for machine forms and for the stylized human figure, manifest in such earlier works as the *Three Women*. Despite the extreme simplification of drawing and modeling, and the use of gray and black instead of natural flesh tones, the cyclist is a far more supple and feminine creature than the stolid women at breakfast in the latter canvas. Léger's fondness for clearly defined patterns is evident throughout the *Big Julie*, in combination with strong colors chosen to show off the shapes of the figures and objects to full advantage. The black background at the left contrasts sharply with the cyclist's gray body, red hat with spiky cockade, and orange suit, against which is silhouetted a big yellow flower with green leaves. At the right, a dark red cross is superimposed on a yellow background. The color and angularity of these shapes serve as foil for the woman's rounded arm and the rhythmic, interlacing curves of her bicycle. The two blue butterflies are gay accents punctuating the black and yellow fields.

Helen M. Franc

LEGER: *Big Julie*
(*La Grande Julie*). 1945.
Oil on canvas, 44 x 50⅛".
The Museum of Modern Art, New York.
Acquired through the
Lillie P. Bliss Bequest

ALBERTO GIACOMETTI was a wiry man, about five feet ten. His face was that of a condottieri; thick, curly brown hair encased his head like medieval headgear. The long, straight, noble nose, the deep creases from cheek to thick-lipped mouth engraved his portrait sharply in my memory. In the movements of his body there was the weight of gravity. In front of his easel, in front of his sculpture, he stood with courage and boldness—his legs, like those of a fighter in a ring, astride and firmly planted. As he worked he would spring forward, step back, scratch his hair.

His studio was one small room, roughly fifteen by twelve feet. I have described it before: "One window takes up a whole wall. Since the studio is on the ground floor and the courtyard is only six feet wide, the light that streams in is gray and dull. The overall impression is of monochromatic grayness. The street outside, the whole quarter is gray. The walls are gray, the sculpture gray and white, interspersed with the sepia accent of wood or the dull glint of bronze. The walls are scratched and scribbled on as though some cave painter had tried to capture images in this cavern. Under the big window is a long table covered with squeezed tubes of paint, palettes, paintbrushes, rags, bottles of turpentine. Like figures, the bottles stand shrouded in layers of dust chipped away from Giacometti's sculpture. Here sculpture and painting mix intimately. On his worktable the two mediums intermingle—turpentine, oil paint, color-soaked plaster, with clay, wire, stone, and bronze. The walls of the studio are covered with drawings, his sketchbooks full. He said, 'I've been fifty thousand times to the Louvre. I have copied everything in drawing, trying to understand. Art is more what one sees than what one reads . . . One does what escapes one most.' "

Giacometti was a man possessed. Time had no meaning in his daily life; he ate and slept as he needed. For him there was no specific hour for any activity, only the time to speak, to create. He created best at night. Sometimes he would work through forty-eight hours without sleep or meals. His best work, he believed, was done after hours and hours of work, when he was so tired that his intelligence had lost control. This is a feeling familiar to many artists, an extraordinary state of trance that can be obtained only through extreme physical fatigue. Then, exhausted, Giacometti would lie on his bed and say, "I don't know. What am I going to do? The work is not coming as it should. I will soon have to look for another métier if it goes on like this."

Alexander Liberman

GIACOMETTI: *The Apple.* 1937.
Oil on canvas, 28¼ x 29⅝".
Private collection, New York

IN GIACOMETTI'S painting, everything is reduced to the simplest means of expression: the heads are so small, the nudes and figures so narrow, just as his brushes were so thin. With two fingers he would hold a long sable brush at its extremity. He would dig it into a tiny layer of gray and white paint. Then with circular, groping movements, as if in a trance, he would shape a small layer of paint into the suggestion of a face in its miniscule form. His eyes would be half-closed, his movements rapid. He smoked incessantly. When he sculptured, there was more abandon in his movement. He seemed to dance around the emerging form.

"Why does one paint or sculpt?" he asked. "It's the need to dominate things, and one can only dominate by understanding. I make a head to understand how I see, not to make a work of art. One must understand through intuition what moves one, and arrive at domination through logic, not through science. Art is not a science . . . No one decides 'I'm going to do sculpture,' or 'I'm going to do painting.' One just does it. It's an absurd activity. One does things through mania, obsession, through an automatic need that escapes the understanding."

Cézanne toward the end of his life expressed the anguish of the truly creative artist. "I have not realized," he wrote. Giacometti was such an artist. He was obsessed with the pursuit of the ideal. Never satisfied, he smashed or discarded much of his work. "I have always failed . . . but I am sure no one can realize that for which he strives! . . . Oh, to be able to say, 'That's it, I cannot do more.'"

Alexander Liberman

THE PORTRAIT appears to me at first as an entanglement of curving lines, commas, closed circles, with lines cutting across—rather in pinks, grays, or blacks, a strange green blending itself in also—a delicate entanglement which he was trying to carry out, and where undoubtedly he lost himself . . . As I withdraw, the face with all its lines appears to me, it imposes itself on me—and according to the phenomena already described, which is inherent in all of Giacometti's figures—it comes to meet me, pounces on me, and darts back into the canvas whence it came, acquiring a terrible presence, reality and relief . . . At this point, the faces painted by Giacometti seem to have accumulated so much life, as if they had not one more second to live, not one more gesture to make, as if they would know Death at last (and not that they have just died), because too much Life would have been poured into them. Seen from twenty meters, each portrait is a small mass of life, hard as a pebble, full as an egg, capable of nourishing without effort a hundred other portraits.

Jean Genet

GIACOMETTI: *Peter Watson.* 1953.
Oil on canvas, 25¾ x 21⅜".
Private collection, New York

Alberto Giacometti, 1958

IN 1954 Picasso began a series of fifteen variations on the theme of Delacroix's master-piece *Les Femmes d'Alger*. This picture had haunted his memory. He had not seen it for years, though he had only to cross the Seine and enter the Louvre to do so. Work-ing from memory, he first painted a composition which in its essentials bore some resemblance to the picture in the Louvre. In quick succession he painted a number of variations, some in monochrome and others with brilliant color.

A suggestion of the tranquil atmosphere of the harem with its ladies seated round a hookah in decorous conversation can still be felt in the first paintings. Soon, how-ever, the scene became more orgiastic. Stripped of their silks and jewelry, the nude bodies of the women are drawn with bold curves indicating the fullness of their breasts and the roundness of their buttocks. One of the two figures in the foreground lies on her side in abandon with her entwined legs lifted in the air, while the other, in contrast richly clothed, sits erect in hieratic indifference. The discreet eroticism of Delacroix's harem has vanished. In Picasso's summary treatment of anatomy, the seduction of the female form is no longer veiled and segregated: it floods the whole picture, affect-ing every corner and opening up the scene from a shadowed confinement to the light of the sun. The more conventional representation of the first paintings made them easy to interpret, but as the series continued Picasso became interested in more abstract qualities of color and form which were the outcome of his former discoveries.

In the last brilliant composition to be painted, reproduced here, Picasso introduced both styles in the same picture. Instead of incongruity he succeeded in achieving an even greater unity, holding the picture together by strong overall patterns of bright color. The two different styles instead of clashing became complementary, offering different versions of the same reality. The more representational seated figure had the effect of spreading its influence over its neighbors, whose forms are less easy to interpret at first sight, humanizing their geometric severity and supplying the key to their metaphorical eroticism.

Roland Penrose

PICASSO: *Women of Algiers.*
1955.

Oil on canvas, 45 x 57⅝".
Collection Mr. and Mrs.
Victor W. Ganz, New York.
See color plate, page 32

CATALOG

IN THE listings below, dates enclosed in parentheses do not appear on the paintings themselves. Dimensions are given in inches and centimeters, height preceding width. The page on which a work is illustrated is given at the end of the entry.

BALLA, Giacomo. Italian, 1871-1958

1 *Dynamism of a Dog on a Leash.* 1912. Oil on canvas, 35⅜ x 43¼″ (89.9 x 109.8 cm). Albright-Knox Art Gallery, Buffalo. Courtesy of George F. Goodyear and The Buffalo Fine Arts Academy. Page 151

BALTHUS (Baltusz Klossowski de Rola). French, born 1908

2 *The Mountain.* (1937). Oil on canvas, 8′ 2¼″ x 11′ 11¾″ (249.5 x 365.1 cm). Private collection, Vaduz. Page 193.

3 *Joan Miró and His Daughter Dolores.* 1937-38. Oil on canvas, 51¼ x 35″ (130.2 x 88.9 cm). The Museum of Modern Art, New York. Abby Aldrich Rockefeller Fund. Page 225

BECKMANN, Max. German, 1884-1950

4 *The Descent from the Cross.* 1917. Oil on canvas, 59½ x 50¾″ (151.2 x 128.9 cm). The Museum of Modern Art, New York. Curt Valentin Bequest. Page 127

BOCCIONI, Umberto. Italian, 1882-1916

5 *The Laugh.* (1911). Oil on canvas, 43⅜ x 57¼″ (110.2 x 145.4 cm). The Museum of Modern Art, New York. Gift of Herbert and Nannette Rothschild. Page 149

BONNARD, Pierre. French, 1867-1947

6 *Boulevard de Clichy.* (c. 1900). Oil on canvas, 25¾ x 36¼″ (65.7 x 92.1 cm). Private collection, New York. Page 229

7 *A Woman with a Cat.* (1912). Oil on canvas, 30¾ x 30¼″ (78.0 x 76.8 cm). Musée National d'Art Moderne, Paris. The Baroness Napoléon Gourgaud Bequest. Page 81

8 *Self-Portrait.* (1945). Oil on canvas, 22 x 18″ (55.8 x 45.7 cm). Collection Mr. and Mrs. Donald S. Stralem, New York. Page 215

BRAQUE, Georges. French, 1882-1963

9 *Piano and Mandola.* (1909-10). Oil on canvas, 36⅛ x 16⅞″ (91.8 x 42.9 cm). The Solomon R. Guggenheim Museum, New York. Page 141

10 *Violin and Palette.* (1909-10). Oil on canvas, 36¼ x 16⅞″ (92.1 x 42.9 cm). The Solomon R. Guggenheim Museum, New York. Page 141

11, *Canephorae.* (1922). Oil on canvas, each 7¼ x 28¾″ (181.0 x 73.0 cm). Musée National d'Art
12 Moderne, Paris. The Baroness Napoléon Gourgaud Bequest. Page 241

13 *The Pedestal Table.* 1935. Oil on canvas, 70¼ x 28½″ (178.4 x 72.4 cm). The San Francisco Museum of Art. Purchased through a gift of W. W. Crocker. Page 249

14 *Still Life with Mandolin.* 1936. Oil on canvas, 38¼ x 51¼″ (97.0 x 130.0 cm). Norton Gallery of Art, West Palm Beach. Page 251

BRAUNER, Victor. Rumanian, 1903-1966

15 *Prelude to a Civilization.* 1954. Encaustic on composition board, 51 x 77″ (129.4 x 195.4 cm). Collection Mr. and Mrs. Jacques Gelman, Mexico City. Page 201

CEZANNE, Paul. French, 1839-1906

16 *Mme Cézanne in a Red Armchair.* (c. 1877). Oil on canvas, 28½ x 22″ (72.5 x 56.0 cm). Museum of Fine Arts, Boston. The Robert Treat Paine, 2nd Bequest. Page 57

17 *L'Estaque.* (1882-85). Oil on canvas, 31½ x 39″ (80.3 x 99.0 cm). The Museum of Modern Art, New York. Gift of William S. Paley, the donor retaining life interest. Page 59

18 *Bathers.* (1882-85). Oil on canvas, 15 x 18″ (38.0 x 45.7 cm). Private collection, Switz. Page 61

19 *Mme Cézanne in a Yellow Chair.* (1893-95). Oil on canvas, 31⅞ x 25½″ (81.0 x 64.8 cm). The Art Institute of Chicago. Wilson L. Mead Fund. Page 65

20 *Bathers.* (c. 1895-1900). Oil on canvas, 10⅝ x 18⅛″ (27.0 x 46.0 cm). The Baltimore Museum of Art. Cone Collection. Page 63

CHAGALL, Marc. French, born Russia 1887

21 *Birthday.* (1915). Oil on cardboard, 31¾ x 39¼″ (80.6 x 99.7 cm). The Museum of Modern Art, New York. Acquired through the Lillie P. Bliss Bequest. Page 183

DE CHIRICO, Giorgio. Italian, born 1888

22 *The Evil Genius of a King.* (1914-15). Oil on canvas, 24 x 19¾″ (61.0 x 50.2 cm). The Museum of Modern Art, New York. Page 181

CORINTH, Lovis. German, 1858-1925

23 *Self-Portrait.* 1924. Oil on canvas, 39⅜ x 31⅝″ (100.0 x 80.3 cm). The Museum of Modern Art, New York. Gift of Curt Valentin. Page 129

DALI, Salvador. Spanish, born 1904

24 *Madonna.* 1958. Oil on canvas, 88⅞ x 75¼″ (223.4 x 191.1 cm). Collection Mr. and Mrs. Henry J. Heinz II, London. Page 203

DEGAS, Hilaire-Germain-Edgar. French, 1834-1917

25 *The Ballet from "Robert le Diable."* 1872. Oil on canvas, 26 x 21⅜″ (66.0 x 54.3 cm). The Metropolitan Museum of Art, New York. The H. O. Havemeyer Collection. Bequest of Mrs. H. O. Havemeyer. Page 39

DELAUNAY, Robert. French, 1885-1941

26 *The Sideboard.* (1916). Oil and encaustic on canvas, 55⅛ x 59½″ (140.0 x 151.0 cm). Musée National d'Art Moderne, Paris. Page 169

DELVAUX, Paul. Belgian, born 1897

27 *Phases of the Moon.* 1939. Oil on canvas, 55 x 63″ (139.7 x 160.0 cm). The Museum of Modern Art, New York. Page 195

DERAIN, André. French, 1880-1954

28 *Henri Matisse.* (1905). Oil on canvas, 18⅛ x 13¾″ (46.1 x 34.9 cm). The Trustees of the Tate Gallery, London. Page 109

29 *View of Collioure.* (1905). Oil on canvas, 23⅝ x 28¾″ (60.0 x 73.0 cm). Musée National d'Art Moderne, Paris. Page 111

30 *The Red Sails.* (1905-06). Oil on canvas, 32 x 39½″ (81.3 x 100.3 cm). Private collection, Houston. Page 113

31 *Francesco de Iturrino.* (1914). Oil on canvas, 36¼ x 25⅝″ (92.0 x 65.0 cm). Musée National d'Art Moderne, Paris. Gift of Mme Geneviève Gallibert. Page 217

DUBUFFET, Jean. French, born 1901

32 *Grand Jazz Band (New Orleans).* 1944. Oil on canvas, 45⅛ x 57⅝″ (114.5 x 146.3 cm). Collection Mr. and Mrs. Gordon Bunshaft, New York. Page 135

DUFY, Raoul. French, 1877-1953

33 *Boats at Dock, Marseilles.* (1908). Oil on canvas, 28¾ x 23⅝" (73.0 x 60.0 cm). Musée National d'Art Moderne, Paris. Bequest of the artist's wife. Page 235

ENSOR, James. Belgian, 1860-1949

34 *Fireworks.* 1887. Oil and encaustic on canvas, 40¼ x 44¼ (102.2 x 112.3 cm). Albright-Knox Art Gallery, Buffalo. George B. and Jenny R. Mathews Fund. Page 67

FEININGER, Lyonel. American, 1871-1956. In Germany 1887-1936

35 *Alley of Trees.* (1914). Oil on canvas, 31¾ x 39¾" (80.7 x 100.9 cm). Private collection, New York. Page 165

GAUGUIN, Paul. French, 1848-1903

36 *Man with an Axe.* 1891. Oil on canvas, 36¼ x 27¼" (92.0 x 69.2 cm). Collection Mr. and Mrs. Alex M. Lewyt, New York. Page 75

37 *The Artist with the Idol.* (c. 1893). Oil on canvas, 17¼ x 12⅞" (43.8 x 32.7 cm). Marion Koogler McNay Art Institute, San Antonio. Bequest of Marion Koogler McNay. Page 211

GIACOMETTI, Alberto. Swiss, 1901-1966

38 *The Apple.* 1937. Oil on canvas, 28¼ x 29⅝" (71.6 x 75.3 cm). Private collection, New York. Page 255

39 *Peter Watson.* 1953. Oil on canvas, 25¾ x 21⅜" (65.7 x 54.2 cm). Private collection, New York. Page 257

VAN GOGH, Vincent. Dutch, 1853-1890

40 *Hospital Corridor.* (1889). Gouache and watercolor on paper, 24⅛ x 18⅝" (61.3 x 47.3 cm). The Museum of Modern Art, New York. Abby Aldrich Rockefeller Bequest. Page 73

GRIS, Juan (José Victoriano González). Spanish, 1887-1927

41 *Man in a Café.* (1912). Oil on canvas, 50⅜ x 34⅝" (127.8 x 88.0 cm). Philadelphia Museum of Art. The Louise and Walter Arensberg Collection. Page 157

42 *Still Life with Pears.* 1913. Oil on canvas, 21¼ x 28¾" (53.9 x 73.0 cm). Collection Mr. and Mrs. Burton Tremaine, Meriden, Conn. Page 159

43 *Violin and Guitar.* (1913). Oil on canvas, 39⅝ x 25⅞" (100.5 x 65.6 cm). Collection Mr. and Mrs. Ralph F. Colin, New York. Page 161

GROSZ, George. American, 1893-1959. Born and died in Germany

44 *Max Herrmann-Neisse.* 1927. Oil on canvas, 23⅜ x 29⅛" (59.4 x 74.0 cm). The Museum of Modern Art, New York. Page 223

JAWLENSKY, Alexey. Russian, 1864-1941

45 *The Gardener.* 1912. Oil on cardboard, 20⅞ x 19⅜" (53.0 x 49.2 cm). Milwaukee Art Center Collection. Gift of Mr. and Mrs. Harry Lynde Bradley. Page 119

KANDINSKY, Wassily. Russian, 1866-1944

46 *Little Pleasures.* 1913. Oil on canvas, 43½ x 47½" (110.5 x 120.6 cm). The Solomon R. Guggenheim Museum, New York. Page 121

KIRCHNER, Ernst Ludwig. German, 1880-1938

47 *Street, Berlin.* (1913). Oil on canvas, 47½ x 35⅞" (120.6 x 91.1 cm). The Museum of Modern Art, New York. Page 123

KLEE, Paul. German, 1879-1940

48 *Man with Top Hat.* 1925. Gouache, pen and ink on paper, 15⅛ x 10⅝" (38.3 x 27.0 cm) (composition), with ½" (1.2 cm) border on cardboard mount painted by the artist. Private collection, New York. Page 189

49 *Portal of a Mosque.* 1931. Watercolor on paper, 14¾ x 11½" (37.3 x 29.1 cm) (composition). Collection Mr. and Mrs. Ralph F. Colin, New York. Page 189

50 *Diana.* 1931. Oil on canvas, 31½ x 23¾" (80.0 x 60.3 cm). Collection Mrs. William A. Bernoudy, St. Louis. Page 191

KOKOSCHKA, Oskar. British, born Austria 1886

51 *Port of Hamburg.* (1951). Oil on canvas, 35¾ x 47½" (90.8 x 120.5 cm). The Museum of Modern Art, New York. Rose Gershwin Fund. Page 133

KUPKA, František (Frank). Czech, 1871-1957. In France from 1895

52 *Mme Kupka among Verticals.* (1911). Oil on canvas, 53⅜ x 33⅝" (135.5 x 85.3 cm). The Museum of Modern Art, New York. Hillman Periodicals Fund. Page 147

LEGER, Fernand. French, 1881-1955

53 *Woman in an Armchair.* (1912). Oil on canvas, 51⅜ x 38⅜" (130.4 x 97.3 cm). Lydia and Harry Lewis Winston Collection (Dr. and Mrs. Barnett Malbin, New York). Page 153

54 *People in a Garden.* 1922. Oil on canvas, 25⅝ x 36¼" (65.1 x 92.0 cm). Collection Mr. and Mrs. Allan D. Emil, New York. Page 239

55 *Big Julie (La Grande Julie).* 1945. Oil on canvas, 44 x 50⅛" (111.8 x 127.3 cm). The Museum of Modern Art, New York. Acquired through the Lillie P. Bliss Bequest. Page 253

MAGRITTE, René. Belgian, 1898-1967

56 *Personal Values.* 1952. Oil on canvas, 31⅝ x 39½" (80.3 x 100.3 cm). Collection Harry Torczyner, New York. Page 199

MALEVICH, Kasimir. Russian, 1878-1935

57 *Scissors Grinder.* (1912). Oil on canvas, 31⅜ x 31⅜" (79.7 x 79.6 cm). Yale University Art Gallery, New Haven, Gift of Collection Société Anonyme. Page 155

58 *Dynamic Suprematism.* (1916). Oil on canvas, 40¼ x 26¼" (102.1 x 66.6 cm). Collection Dr. Armand Hammer, Los Angeles. Page 173

MANET, Edouard. French, 1832-1883

59 *A Boy with a Sword.* (1861). Oil on canvas, 51⅝ x 36¾" (131.1 x 93.4 cm). The Metropolitan Museum of Art, New York. Gift of Erwin Davis. Page 37

60 *Women at the Races.* 1865. Oil on canvas, 16⅝ x 12⅝" (42.2 x 32.0 cm). Cincinnati Art Museum. Frontispiece

61 *House at Rueil.* 1882. Oil on canvas, 36½ x 29" (92.7 x 73.5 cm). National Gallery of Victoria, Melbourne. Felton Bequest. Page 41

MARC, Franz. German, 1880-1916

62 *Animals in a Landscape.* 1914. Oil on canvas, 43⅜ x 39¼" (110.1 x 99.7 cm). The Detroit Institute of Arts. Gift of Robert Hudson Tannahill. Page 167

MATISSE, Henri. French, 1869-1954

63 *The Guitarist.* (1903). Oil on canvas, 22 x 15⅜" (55.8 x 38.8 cm). Collection Mr. and Mrs. Ralph F. Colin, New York. Page 85

64 *The Young Sailor.* 1906. Oil on canvas, 39⅜ x 31⅞" (100.0 x 81.0 cm). Collection Mr. and Mrs. Jacques Gelman, Mexico City. Page 87

65 *View of Collioure.* (1908). Oil on canvas, 35⅞ x 24⅞" (91.0 x 63.0 cm). Collection Mr. and Mrs. Jacques Gelman, Mexico City. Page 89

66 *Girl with Green Eyes.* (1909). Oil on canvas, 26 x 20" (66.0 x 50.7 cm). San Francisco Museum of Art. Harriet Lane Levy Bequest. Page 91

67 *Woman on a High Stool.* (1913-14). Oil on canvas, 57⅞ x 37⅝" (147.0 x 95.5 cm). The Museum of Modern Art, New York. Gift of Mr. and Mrs. Samuel A. Marx, the latter retaining life interest. Page 93

68 *Montalban.* (1918). Oil on canvas, 29½ x 36½" (74.9 x 92.7 cm). Private collection, France. Page 95

69 *The Artist and His Model.* (1919). Oil on canvas, 23⅝ x 28¾" (60.0 x 73.0 cm). Collection Dr. Ruth M. Bakwin, New York. Page 97

70 *Two Rays.* 1920. Oil on canvas. 36¼ x 28¾" (92.0 x 73.0 cm). Norton Gallery of Art, West Palm Beach. Page 99

71 *Checker Game and Piano Music.* (1923). Oil on canvas, 29 x 36½" (73.6 x 92.7 cm). Collection Mr. and Mrs. Alexandre P. Rosenberg, New York. Page 101

72 *Dancer and Armchair.* 1942. Oil on canvas, 19⅞ x 25⅞" (50.4 x 65.8 cm). Private collection, France. Page 103

73 *Large Interior in Red.* 1948. Oil on canvas, 57½ x 38¼" (146.0 x 97.0 cm). Musée National d'Art Moderne, Paris. Page 105

MIRO, Joan. Spanish, born 1893

74 *Self-Portrait.* 1917. Oil on canvas, 24 x 19⅝" (61.0 x 49.8 cm). The Bragaline Collection, New York. Page 221

75 *Maternity.* 1924. Oil on canvas, 36⅜ x 28¾" (92.3 x 73.0 cm). Private collection, London. Page 185

76 *Painting.* 1933. Oil on canvas, 68½ x 77¼" (174.0 x 196.2 cm). The Museum of Modern Art, New York. Gift of the Advisory Committee. Page 187

MODIGLIANI, Amedeo, Italian, 1884-1920

77 *Portrait of a Man.* (1917). Oil on canvas, 39½ x 25⅝" (100.3 x 65.0 cm). National Gallery of Victoria, Melbourne. Felton Bequest. Page 219

78 *Reclining Nude.* (1917). Oil on canvas, 25½ x 39½" (64.8 x 100.3 cm). Collection Richard S. Zeisler, New York. Page 237

MONDRIAN, Piet. Dutch, 1872-1944

79 *Color Planes in Oval.* (1914?). Oil on canvas, 42⅜ x 31" (107.6 x 78.8 cm). The Museum of Modern Art, New York

MONET, Claude. French, 1840-1926

80 *Water Lilies and Japanese Bridge.* (1899). Oil on canvas, 35⅝ x 35⅜" (90.5 x 89.7 cm). The Art Museum, Princeton University, Princeton. From the Collection of William Church Osborn, Class of 1883, Trustee of Princeton University (1914-51), President of the Metropolitan Museum of Art (1941-47). Given by His Family. Page 47

81 *Water Lilies.* 1907. Oil on canvas, 35½ x 28½" (90.1 x 72.4 cm). Lydia and Harry Lewis Winston Collection (Dr. and Mrs. Barnett Malbin, New York). Page 49

82 *Venice, The Doge's Palace.* 1908. Oil on canvas, 32 x 39⅝" (81.2 x 100.6 cm). The Brooklyn Museum. Gift of A. Augustus Healy. Page 51

83 *Still Life with a Basket of Eggs.* (c. 1910). Oil on canvas, 29⅜ x 36⅞" (74.6 x 93.6 cm). Collection Mrs. Lloyd Bruce Wescott, Rosemont, N.J. Page 53

MUNCH, Edvard. Norwegian, 1863-1944

84 *The Voice.* 1893. Oil on canvas, 34½ x 42½" (87.5 x 107.8 cm). Museum of Fine Arts, Boston. Ernest Wadsworth Longfellow Fund. Page 77

NOLDE, Emil (Emil Hansen). Danish, born Germany. 1867-1956

85 *Russian Peasants.* (1915). Oil on canvas, 29 x 35½" (73.4 x 90.0 cm). The Museum of Modern Art, New York. The Matthew T. Mellon Foundation Fund. Page 125

PICASSO, Pablo. Spanish, 1881-1973

86 *Landscape, La Rue des Bois.* (1908). Oil on canvas, 39⅝ x 32⅛" (100.6 x 81.6 cm). Collection Mr. and Mrs. David Rockefeller, New York. Page 139

87 *Portrait of a Woman.* (1910). Oil on canvas, 39¾ x 32¼" (100.8 x 81.9 cm). Collection Mrs. Gilbert W. Chapman, New York. Page 143

88 *Bottle, Glass, and Fork.* (1912). Oil on canvas, 28¾ x 21¼" (73.0 x 54.0 cm). The Cleveland Museum of Art. Purchase, Leonard C. Hanna, Jr. Bequest. Page 145

89 *Portrait of a Young Girl.* 1914. Oil on canvas, 51¼ x 38¼" (130.0 x 97.0 cm). Musée National d'Art Moderne, Paris. Bequest of Georges Salles. Page 163

90 *Studio with Plaster Head.* 1925. Oil on canvas, 38⅝ x 51⅝" (97.9 x 131.1 cm). The Museum of Modern Art, New York. Page 243

91 *The Studio.* 1927-28. Oil on canvas, 59 x 91" (149.9 x 231.2 cm). The Museum of Modern Art, New York. Gift of Walter P. Chrysler, Jr. Page 245

92 *Women of Algiers.* 1955. Oil on canvas, 45 x 57⅝" (114.3 x 146.2 cm). Collection Mr. and Mrs. Victor W. Ganz, New York. Page 259

REDON, Odilon. French, 1840-1916

93 *Death.* (After 1905). Oil on cardboard, 22⅜ x 18¾" (56.7 x 47.6 cm). Collection Mrs. Bertram Smith, New York. Page 179

RENOIR, Pierre Auguste. French, 1841-1919

94 *Monet Painting in His Garden.* (c. 1874). Oil on canvas, 18⅜ x 23½" (46.7 x 59.7 cm). Wadsworth Atheneum, Hartford, Conn. Bequest of Anne Parrish Titzell. Page 43

95 *Venice, The Doge's Palace.* 1881. Oil on canvas, 21⅜ x 25¾" (54.2 x 65.4 cm). Sterling and Francine Clark Art Institute, Williamstown, Mass. Page 45

96 *Child in White.* 1883. Oil on canvas, 24¼ x 19¾" (61.7 x 50.1 cm). The Art Institute of Chicago. Mr. and Mrs. Martin A. Ryerson Collection. Page 207

ROUAULT, Georges. French, 1871-1958

97 *Girl at a Mirror.* 1906. Watercolor on cardboard, 27⅝ x 20⅞" (70.0 x 53.0 cm). Musée National d'Art Moderne, Paris. Page 115

98 *Two Prostitutes.* 1906. Watercolor and pastel on cardboard, 26½ x 24¼" (67.3 x 61.6 cm). Collection E. M. Bakwin. Page 115

ROUSSEAU, Henri. French, 1844-1910

99 *The Merry Jesters.* (c. 1906). Oil on canvas, 57⅜ x 44⅝" (145.7 x 113.3 cm). Philadelphia Museum of Art. The Louise and Walter Arensberg Collection. Page 177

SCHMIDT-ROTTLUFF, Karl. German, born 1884

100 *Pharisees.* 1912. Oil on canvas, 29⅞ x 40½" (75.9 x 102.9 cm). The Museum of Modern Art, New York. Gertrud A. Mellon Fund

SEURAT, Georges Pierre. French, 1859-1891.

101 *Port-en-Bessin: The Outer Harbor.* (1888). Oil on canvas, 21¼ x 25¾" (54.0 x 65.3 cm). The St. Louis Art Museum. Page 69

SEVERINI, Gino. Italian, 1883-1966

102 *Armored Train in Action.* (1915). Oil on canvas, 46 x 34½" (116.8 x 87.6 cm). Collection Richard S. Zeisler, New York. Page 171

SIGNAC, Paul. French, 1863-1935

103 *Gas Tanks at Clichy.* 1886. Oil on canvas, 25½ x 31⅞" (64.8 x 80.9 cm). National Gallery of Victoria, Melbourne. Felton Bequest. Page 71

SOUTINE, Chaim. French, born Lithuania. 1893-1943

104 *Chartres Cathedral.* (1933). Oil on wood, 36⅜ x 19¾" (92.3 x 50.0 cm). The Museum of Modern Art, New York. Gift of Mrs. Lloyd Bruce Wescott. Page 247

105 *Alley of Trees.* (1936). Oil on canvas, 30⅛ x 27⅜" (76.3 x 69.3 cm). Collection Lady Harlech, London. Page 131

TANGUY, Yves. American, born France. 1900-1955. To U.S.A. 1939

106 *Fear.* (1949). Oil on canvas, 60 x 40" (152.3 x 101.6 cm). Whitney Museum of American Art, New York. Page 197

TOULOUSE-LAUTREC, Henri de. French, 1864-1901

107 *M. Boileau in a Café.* (1893). Gouache on cardboard, 31½ x 25⅝" (80.0 x 65.0 cm). The Cleveland Museum of Art. Hinman B. Hurlbut Collection. Page 209

UTRILLO, Maurice. French, 1883-1955

108 *Chartres Cathedral.* (1913). Oil on canvas, 36⅜ x 25¾" (92.4 x 65.4 cm). Collection Mr. and Mrs. Alex M. Lewyt, New York. Page 247

VLAMINCK, Maurice de. French, 1876-1958

109 *Tugboat at Chatou.* (1906). Oil on canvas, 19¾ x 25¾" (50.1 x 65.4 cm). Collection Mr. and Mrs. John Hay Whitney, New York. Page 117

VUILLARD, Edouard. French, 1868-1940

110 *Girls Walking.* (1891). Oil on canvas, 32 x 25⅝" (81.2 x 65.1 cm). Private collection, New York. Page 231

111 *Self-Portrait.* (1892). Oil on canvas, 14⅜ x 11⅛" (36.4 x 28.2 cm). Collection Mr. and Mrs. Ralph F. Colin, New York. Page 233

112 *Family at Table.* (c. 1897). Oil on board, 19½ x 28" (49.5 x 71.1 cm). Private collection, New York. Page 79

113 *Mme Arthur Fontaine.* (c. 1900). Oil on cardboard, 24⅞ x 22½" (63.1 x 57.1 cm). Private collection, New York. Page 213

PHOTOGRAPH CREDITS

This catalog has been made possible only through the cooperation and contributions of many individuals and organizations. We are grateful to the following authors who have graciously provided commentaries (indicated by page number) for this project:

Susana Leval, pages 68, 74, 120, 152, 164, 166, 168, 202, 210, 238.
Roland Penrose, page 142.
Stuart Preston, pages 52, 58, 78, 80, 110, 112, 212, 214, 216, 228, 230, 232, 234.
Bernice Rose, page 200.
John Russell, page 192.
Virginia Spate, pages 60-62, 146.

ACKNOWLEDGMENTS

Commentaries by the following authors have been excerpted or adapted from works originally published by The Museum of Modern Art:

Alfred H. Barr, Jr.: Page 172, from *Cubism and Abstract Art*, by Alfred H. Barr, Jr.; copyright © 1936 by The Museum of Modern Art, New York; copyright renewed 1964. Page 66, from *Masters of Modern Art*, edited by Alfred H. Barr, Jr.; second edition, 1954. Pages 86, 90, 98, 100, 102, from *Matisse: His Art and His Public*, by Alfred H. Barr, Jr.; copyright © 1951 by The Museum of Modern Art, New York. Page 242, from *Picasso: Fifty Years of His Art*, by Alfred H. Barr, Jr.; copyright © 1946 by The Museum of Modern Art, New York; copyright renewed 1974.

Helen M. Franc: Pages 108, 186, 194, 224, 252, from *An Invitation to See: 125 Paintings from The Museum of Modern Art*, by Helen M. Franc; copyright © 1973 by The Museum of Modern Art, New York.

Lawrence Gowing: Pages 96, 104, from *Henri Matisse: 64 Paintings*, by Lawrence Gowing; copyright © 1966 by The Museum of Modern Art, New York.

Lucy R. Lippard: Pages 122, 124, 148, from *De Cézanne à Miró*, introduction by Monroe Wheeler, commentaries by Lucy R. Lippard; copyright © 1968 by The Museum of Modern Art, New York. Page 92, from *The School of Paris: Paintings from the Florene May Schoenborn and Samuel A. Marx Collection*, preface by Alfred H. Barr, Jr., introduction by James Thrall Soby, notes by Lucy R. Lippard; copyright © 1965 by The Museum of Modern Art, New York.

William C. Seitz: Pages 46, 48, 50, from *Monet: Seasons and Moments*, by William C. Seitz; The Museum of Modern Art, New York, 1960.

James Thrall Soby: Page 114, from *Georges Rouault: Paintings and Prints*, by James Thrall Soby; copyright © 1945 by The Museum of Modern Art, New York. Pages 156, 158, 160, from *Juan Gris*, by James Thrall Soby; The Museum of Modern Art, New York, 1958.

James Johnson Sweeney: Page 182, from *Marc Chagall*, by James Johnson Sweeney; copyright © 1946 by The Museum of Modern Art, New York. Page 188, from *Paul Klee*, articles by Alfred H. Barr, Jr., James Johnson Sweeney, and Julia and Lyonel Feininger; copyright © 1941 by The Museum of Modern Art, New York.

Joshua C. Taylor: Pages 150, 170, from *Futurism*, by Joshua C. Taylor; The Museum of Modern Art, New York, 1961.

Monroe Wheeler: Pages 130, 246, from *Soutine*, by Monroe Wheeler; copyright © 1950 by The Museum of Modern Art, New York.

We are grateful to the museums, galleries, and publishers responsible for the original appearance of the commentaries by the following authors:

Dennis Adrian: Page 66, from *James Ensor: The Early Work*, text by Dennis Adrian; Allan Frumkin Gallery, New York, c. 1961-63.

John Ashbery: Page 196, from *Yves Tanguy*, text by John Ashbery; Acquavella Galleries, Inc., New York, 1974.

Douglas Cooper: Pages 240, 248, 250, from *Braque: The Great Years*, by Douglas Cooper; The Art Institute of Chicago, 1972. Page 140, from *The Cubist Epoch*, by Douglas Cooper; Phaidon Publishers, Inc., New York, 1971.

Pierre Courthion: Page 68, from *Seurat*, by Pierre Courthion; Harry N. Abrams, Inc., New York, 1968.

Marcel Duchamp: Pages 88, 138, 180, from *The Collection of the Société Anonyme: The Museum of Modern Art 1920*, by Katherine S. Dreier and Marcel Duchamp; copyright © 1950 by the Associates in Fine Arts at Yale University; Yale University Art Gallery, New Haven, 1950.

Jean Genet: Page 256, from *L'Atelier d'Alberto Giacometti*, by Jean Genet; Barbezat, Décines, 1963.

Robert L. Herbert: Page 70, from *Neo-Impressionism*, by Robert L. Herbert; The Solomon R. Guggenheim Foundation, New York, 1968.

Ursula Hoff and Margaret Plant: Pages 40, 218, from *National Gallery of Victoria: Painting, Drawing, Sculpture*, by Ursula Hoff and Margaret Plant; copyright © 1968 by The Trustees of the National Gallery of Victoria; F. W. Cheshire Publishing Pty. Ltd., Melbourne.

Sherman E. Lee: Page 208, from *A Colorslide Tour of the Cleveland Museum of Art*, with Sherman E. Lee; copyright © 1960 by Harry N. Abrams, Inc., New York.

John Maxon: Pages 42, 206, from *Paintings by Renoir*, text by John Maxon; The Art Institute of Chicago, 1973. Page 64, from *The Art Institute of Chicago*, by John Maxon; copyright © 1970 by Thames and Hudson, London; Thames and Hudson, London, and Harry N. Abrams, Inc., New York, 1972.

Alexander Liberman: Pages 254, 256, from *The Artist in His Studio*, by Alexander Liberman; copyright © by Alexander Liberman; Viking Press, New York, 1960.

Katharine B. Neilson: Page 154, from *Selected Paintings and Sculpture from the Yale University Art Gallery*, introduction by Andrew Carnduff Ritchie, commentaries by Katharine B. Neilson; copyright © 1972 by Yale Univertsity; Yale University Press, New Haven and London, 1972.

Paul Nougé: Page 198, from *Surrealism*, by Julien Levy; copyright © 1936 by The Black Sun Press, New York.

Roland Penrose: Page 184, from *Miró*, by Roland Penrose; copyright © 1970 by Thames and Hudson, London; Thames and Hudson, London, and Harry N. Abrams, Inc., New York, 1970. Page 258, from *Picasso: His Life and Work*, by Roland Penrose; copyright © 1958 by Roland Penrose; Victor Gollancz, Ltd., London, 1958, and Harper and Row, New York, 1959.

John Rewald: Pages 116, 176, from *The John Hay Whitney Collection*, text by John Rewald; The Tate Gallery, London, 1960.

Margaretta M. Salinger: Pages 36, 38, from *French Paintings: A Catalogue of the Collection of The Metropolitan Museum of Art*; vol. III, *XIX-XX Centuries*, by Charles Sterling and Margaretta M. Salinger; copyright © 1967 by The Metropolitan Museum of Art, New York.